Confucius Meets Piaget

For information and additional copies contact:

Jonathan F. Borden
Seoul Foreign School, 55 Yonhi Dong
Seoul, Korea 120-113
Ph: (82-2) 330-3240
Fax: (82-2) 335-1857

Email: JFBorden@hotmail.com
         jborden@sfs.or.kr

or through

Seoul Foreign School
55 Yonhi Dong
Seoul, Korea 120-113

Cover design by Joan Lueth

Printed in Seoul, Republic of Korea

Confucius Meets Piaget:

An Educational Perspective on Ethnic Korean Children and Their Parents

Second Edition

Jonathan F. Borden

RUSSIA

MONGOLIA

Manchuria

N. Korea

CHINA

S. Korea

JAPAN

PACIFIC OCEAN

MAP OF NORTHEAST ASIA — 2003

DEDICATION

To my sons Eugene and Dan, who have taught me so much
about what it means to be a kid growing up as a foreigner,
and to my number one encourager and inspiration,
my wife Soon-ok.

TABLE OF CONTENTS

AUTHOR'S NOTE

I would like to thank the many hundreds of teachers who have helped over the years with input and insights, as well as some dear friends and co-workers who have done some of the less pleasant nitty-gritty work of putting this book together. They have been constant encouragement and inspiration. I also thank all the children and their parents with names like Park, Kim, and Lee whom I have grown to love and respect over the years. Finally, I thank the best intercultural teacher anyone could every have, my wife Soon-ok.

J. Borden

The author welcomes the reader's comments, ideas, and perspectives. It is only through sharing and discussion that the educational community can continue to grow in understanding of the important educational questions and issues facing it today.

Confucius Meets Piaget:

An Educational Perspective on Ethnic Korean Children and Their Parents

"They will work hard, they will give you honor, they will over-achieve, they will push for extra points in their grade, their behavior will confound you and sometimes frustrate you. But at the end of the day you will have a sense of accomplishment and pride in the education that has happened in your classroom."

- a teacher in an international school in Seoul

What measure of truth is there in this statement? Is it simply a stereotypical, biased comment by a teacher who has had his or her share of good and bad days teaching ethnic Korean students? Perhaps. But nearly anyone who has worked with or taught more than a few ethnic Korean students has shared similar feelings and attitudes. At any meeting of international teachers, when the subject of ethnic Korean students comes up, a litany of stories, testimonies, frustrations, and wonder emerges. It is hoped that this book will help separate fact from fiction, and in doing so add some clarity and professional perspective to this ongoing and fascinating discussion.

INTRODUCTION

The opinions and observations shared in this book are the result of impressions formed over more than twenty-five years of experience working with ethnic Korean students, their parents, and their teachers in an international school in Seoul, Korea. Professional reading has also provided a good deal of background material. Living in a bi-cultural family has given me both a close-up look at Korean values and educational priorities as well as a critical eye towards what might too often be a "foreigner's stereotype" of Korea and Koreans. This book admittedly presents my own American perspective, although it has received a positive reaction from Koreans of various degrees of Westernization. Of course, I take full responsibility for all that is contained on these pages.

This book was the outgrowth of a number of events — it had its genesis in the preparation of a paper written at Walden University in the spring of 1994 entitled "Understanding Korean-American Students and their Parents." The first two versions of this book, one entitled *Understanding Korean-American Students and Their Parents* (1994) and a much expanded version with the slightly different title and focus *Understanding Ethnic Korean Children and Their Parents: An Educational Perspective* (1997), were also the bases for presentations made at the international school administrators' conference of the East Asia Council of Overseas Schools (EARCOS) in Bangkok in the fall of 1997, the international teachers' conference of Near East/South Asia Council of Overseas Schools (NESA) in Bangkok the spring of 1998, and at the Missionary Kids Overseas Schools (MCOS) conference held in Seoul in the fall of 1999, as well as at various educational conferences and international schools in Korea and China since 1994. Whenever and wherever this presentation has been made, it has generated a good deal of discussion — some positive, some negative. But it *has* generated discussion of a phenomenon that had been informally recognized in staff rooms and faculty meetings in international schools around the world for a number of years, but which was avoided in truly public discussion for fear of appearing to be culturally biased or ethnically insensitive. Once in the open, however, teachers begin to share their experiences and frustrations, but more importantly their ideas — strategies of how they have found success working with ethnic Korean students and parents, and ideas of how to better understand and teach them. The true benefactors of this discussion have been the children and parents themselves — for to understand someone more deeply is to respect them more fully. For teachers this understanding means being able to forge relationships with students and families that result in these children becoming truly international children, or at least being able to negotiate the tricky waters that run between national pride and internationalism.

Before we go any further it would be valuable to define the term "ethnic Korean." This term means different things to different people, depending on their own past experience. In its most basic definition it means any person whose forebears came originally from Korea. For the purposes of this book, which is directed at non-Korean teachers teaching in international schools within and outside of Korea, there are three main groups of ethnic Korean children with whom Western teachers come into contact: 1) "hyphenated Koreans" such as Korean-Americans, Korean-British, or Korean-Australians, children brought up outside of Korea and who may "look" Asian on the outside but have been totally acculturated into the Western culture in which they live and

3

are citizens; 2) ethnic Korean children who have spent a significant part of their childhood outside of Korea, but are now living in Korea and attending either Korean or international schools, but whose futures most likely lie outside of Korea; and 3) Korean nationals who are attending international schools outside of Korea due to their parents' work or assignment; normally such children's "core culture" is Korean and they are planning to return to Korea for higher education and for adult life. This last group has been growing very rapidly in numbers since 1990.

It should be noted that this book deals primarily with children of South Korean heritage. While certainly there are strong cultural similarities between The Republic of Korea (democratic South) and the Democratic Peoples' Republic of Korea (communist North), the impact of fifty years of communist rule and recent years of harsh famine and economic collapse have changed Koreans north of the DMZ to the core, just as fifty years of developing democratic institutions and raging capitalism have changed the minds and hearts of those in the South. How different the children of these two nations will be in international schools in the future is unknown; perhaps in a brighter day when the North finally opens itself to the world and more than a trickle of loyal diplomats from there begin to travel around the world will we find out. Many in both Koreas eagerly look forward to that day.

This book has been written in an attempt to help teachers and others who work with ethnic Korean children to better understand them by understanding their backgrounds – their values, their histories, their families, and their goals for the future. One might fairly ask, "Why would we single out children of Korean descent any more than we would children of German or Chinese descent? What would make them different from any American or British or Cana-

4

dian or German child? Aren't distinctions such as this racism at its fullest?" The answers to these questions depend on who is asking them, and which type of ethnic Korean child described above is being discussed. Teachers in North America or Europe, for example, (or in international schools in Korea) who have ethnic Korean children in their classes who seem "Western" in culture may be the first to ask. For them, the answer is that these children are the products of their parents' upbringing as well as of their own experience in the West. As Koreans are among the very newest of ethnic groups to emigrate in large numbers to the United States, they are still affected much more strongly by their native culture than, say, German or Scottish Americans. Koreans as an American immigrant group have had a much shorter time to acculturate, most having emigrated since the late 1970's. U.S. Census data from 1980 showed that only 16% of those who classified themselves as ethnically Korean were born in the U. S. (*Handbook for Teaching Korean-American Students*). Therefore, even by the time of this publication in 2003, any children born since 1980 and brought up in the U.S. would not yet have children of their own in school, and would themselves be children of emigrants. Thus, all except 16% of ethnic Koreans in the United States would necessarily be immigrants or children of immigrants, and would therefore be strongly influenced by their own or their parents' native Korean cultural background.

The answer to the question of why we might focus on ethnic Korean students is simpler for teachers of ethnic Korean students in international schools. These students are different from other students for the same reasons that students of other backgrounds are different from them – they have parents from a different culture and in many cases have attended school in yet a third culture, and thus have different

5

academic and social habits, characteristics, and attributes. That is only natural; differences such as these make teaching in international schools rewarding and fun!

Finally, it should be emphasized that whenever any group is described in general terms, there are necessarily many individuals who do not conform to all, or even to some, generalities. One challenge that faces the reader is to sort out what information and insights shared here are applicable to students in his or her classroom. Some information may fit perfectly and be of immediate help. Other thoughts may seem totally out of synch with the reader's experience. Such is the nature of the wide range of backgrounds of these children: each has a unique family history and personality that deeply affect the development of cultural identity. Thus, accepting the inevitability of being "proven" wrong by those who can provide legitimate exceptions to the characteristics described in this book, I'll forge ahead hoping that many readers will be able to better understand in some small or significant way the ethnic Korean students found in their classrooms on Monday morning.

Jonathan F. Borden, Ph. D.
Seoul, Korea
Spring 2003

PART I: WHERE ARE THEY COMING FROM?

CHAPTER I: CULTURAL STEREOTYPING OR ANTHROPOLOGY?

At the beginning of the Twenty-first Century, millennia-old issues of ethnicity, racism, prejudice, and discrimination are clashing head to head with large and rapid migrations of varied peoples brought on by war, famine, and economic or political hardship. Our world is rapidly being contracted in time, if not in space, by high-speed transportation and instant communication. It is being torn apart by the conflicting movements of "one-world-ism" on one hand and those of nationalism, ethnic pride, religion and regionalism on the other. Forces such as international commerce, multi-national corporations, the Internet, CNN, increasing numbers of multi-national military operations, and the lower cost of travel are all making the world more homogeneous. Each of these forces brings cultures and individuals into closer contact than ever before in history. As people of various cultures and backgrounds have come in contact and inevitable clashes have occurred, the natural tendency towards conflict has thankfully been most often balanced by an equally strong impulse to understand one another and to get along, if only for reasons of economic profit and human survival. This has led to necessary tolerance of others and their customs, religions,

7

beliefs, and value systems. It has also led to the politically correct belief, at least in the United States, that "deep down inside, we're all the same" and that seeming differences are really only a veneer of fascinating variations in language, clothing, food, and music. Like the iceberg that is only one-tenth out of the water, however, language, clothing, food, and music are only the very visible (and usually quite beautiful and interesting) aspects of a culture. As anyone who has lived in a culture other than his or her own for any more than a quick tourist visit knows, however, unfortunately the other nine-tenths of the cultural iceberg are hidden, and are its real life and soul. When we live in a culture other than our own, we soon come to the realization that despite what we might have been taught as children, everybody isn't "just the same under the skin." There are deep, serious, and critical areas of values and identity that are very different from one culture to another. The fact that these are hidden makes them danger-ous and unexpected, and can send us into culture shock and onto the next flight out! These hidden values and critical be-liefs are the parts of the cultural iceberg that can catch us in unexpectedly cold and rough water, rip into our senses of se-curity and propriety, and send us to the bottom before we know what hit us. (For more on the iceberg analogy, see L. Robert Kohls's *Survival Kit for Overseas Living*. 3rd ed.).

Let's look at some of these "under the surface" differ-ences between East Asian and Western cultures. The chart on the next page is purposely simplistic and is not meant in any way to categorize or simplify extremely complex and diverse cultural groups.

If we look at each of the social characteristics listed in the left-hand column, we do not see absolutes, but tendencies. For example, we certainly find examples of both democracies

Value System	European-based (Judeo-Christian)	East Asian-Based (Buddhist/ Confucian)
Political Tradition	Democratic	Totalitarian/ authoritarian
Gender bias	Male-dominated/ deference to females	Male-dominated/ deference to males
Personal/ group Orientation	Individualistic	Group Oriented
Value Priorities	Honesty	Relationships
Political History	History of Domination	History of Subservience
Space Orientation	Space-rich	Space-poor
Geopolitical Stance	Internationalism	Isolationism: The Hermit Kingdom

COMPARING VALUE SYSTEMS

and totalitarian regimes in both the East and the West. However, we find more of a political tradition (at least in the last two hundred years) of a move towards democratic institutions in the West, while in South Korea, for example, moves towards democracy have only been seriously attempted since the early 1990's. More important for us, however, is the realization that cultural variations in the concepts of democracy and individual rights exist not only in politics, but in the family, as well. For example, the idea that children have opinions that are real and important is not given much credence in most Korean families. Taking another characteristic, that of the sensitive area of Value Priorities (about which a good deal more will be discussed later) it is important to emphasize that honesty is certainly important in Korea, just as relationships are important to Westerners. However, when the two values come into conflict in the West, honesty more often than not (at least ideally) comes out on top. Famous fables of the greatest American heroes speak to this. Most Americans, for example, would name George Washington and Abe Lincoln as among the greatest U. S. presidents. It is no coincidence that a commonly known quote (however mythical) of young George Washington, when asked about the felled cherry tree, is "I cannot tell a lie." And what is Lincoln's nickname but "*Honest* Abe?" Richard Nixon's fall from America's grace was not so much a result of his involvement in a criminal act; it was his lack of honesty to the American people in dealing with it that sealed his political fate. Honesty is at the core of American values, even if it is often ignored or abused. On the other hand, contemporary Korean news is rife with stories of dishonesty resulting from giving in to the urge not to break or strain a *relationship*. Korean heroes such as Admiral Yi Sunshin or patriot Yoo Kwan-soon are famous for their intense loyalty to the nation, that is, to their *relationship* to the ethnic

10

and national group. (More on this later.) Readers are encouraged to examine each of the general characteristics and tendencies found on the chart to see in which examples they might find agreement or differences, based on personal experience.

In order to understand any culture and learn what makes its individuals "tick," then, we have to look below the surface to see how the value systems that underpin the society operate. When this is done in a positive, neutral, and nonjudgmental way, it is called anthropology. When it is done from a near-sighted, judgmental, or nationalistic perspective, however, it is correctly called stereotyping. The anthropological comment that "Korean culture places a higher importance on education than do some other cultures," for example, can be twisted to a stereotypical "All Koreans care about is that their child goes to Harvard!" This is, of course, what we want to avoid.

> *In order to understand any culture and learn what makes its individuals "tick," then, we have to look below the surface to see how the value systems that underpin the society operate.*

Because of an understandable hesitancy to be viewed as being prejudiced, we often opt not to consider differences between peoples (beyond the food, clothing, language, and music level) at all. This is particularly true in the United States where many still believe in the dream of the happy melting pot "with liberty and justice for all" and where political correctness reigns supreme. On the other hand, each culture, including that of the United States, is quite comfortable stereotyping itself. For example, citizens of the United States will tell the visitor that they pride themselves on their "independent American spirit" and "strong egalitarian tradition." Stating such generalities begs such questions then, as "Do all U.S. citizens exercise the same degree of independence?" "Do all desire the same amount of independence?" "Do the words of the Declaration of Independence ring true for all?" Of course not, we answer. However, someone attempting to answer the question "What makes U.S. Americans tick?" would be ill-prepared unless 1) a solid look at the historical, cultural, and geographic background of the nation was not taken, and 2) an understanding of the independent and self-reliant spirit that guides much public and private decision-making in the nation was not achieved.

Similarly, the British might consider themselves to be, within their historical and geographic context "formal," or Australians "informal," or Japanese "polite." We are often very content to stereotype our own cultures. In this context, and with the understood danger of being labeled as being biased or even bigoted, a look at the historical, cultural, and educational backgrounds of ethnic Korean children and their parents (or those of any other cultural group) is appropriate in an honest attempt to better understand the children we might teach. As long as we are willing and able to distinguish between the general characteristics of a cultural group and those of its individual members (personal history, heredity, etc.), we are on safe ground.

To understand ethnic Korean children, whether they are children of immigrants to the West, children who happen to hold a foreign passport and find themselves in international schools in Korea, or "overseas Koreans" living temporarily outside of Korea, we must first understand the parents who hold the values, habits, and world outlook that mold their children. Specifically, we are going to examine the historical, cultural, educational backgrounds that many of these parents share with one another. We will also look at individual life experiences that create exceptions to these generalities. The children of these parents are in our schools, and they bring the influences of their parents' background with them to school each morning. Some of these characteristics make them top students, friendly and positive kids who are a teacher's idea of a dream class. On the other hand, some characteristics can threaten to make us question the core values of our schools, institute draconian rules against our better judgment, or just become disappointed and jaded.

TIME TO WRITE...

Perhaps a good way to begin is for the reader to take a few minutes and jot down his or her own impressions of ethnic Korean students he or she has taught. Be totally honest with yourself — no one is going to check! Make two lists: write down those endearing characteristics of ethnic Korean children you have taught that seem to distinguish them from other students. Then (be honest, now!) write down those characteristics which are less endearing. Try to depend on your own experience rather than on what "everybody knows" is true. Then make note of any questions you have about your ethnic Korean students – ask why they are the way they are. You might not find the specific answers to your questions in this book, but you might gain some insight into what makes them "tick." Jot down your lists and questions in the back of this book, and take a look at them from time to time. As you read, hopefully connections will begin to appear, and although you will still have some questions at the end, it all may at least *begin* to make sense.

13

CHAPTER II: HISTORICAL BACKGROUND

The Nation of Korea

Each of us is to a great extent a product of the history of our homeland. Korea and Koreans are no exception. Korea has a very long and proud history. Artifacts of Paleolithic age have been found in Korea, dating habitation of the Korean peninsula back more than 30,000 years. History in the form of artwork reaches at least as far back as 4000 B. C. A highly developed, artistic society evolved over the next five millennia. A specifically Korean culture, with its own language, literature, social structure, government, religion, music, cuisine, and culture developed, related to yet distinct from neighboring Chinese, Mongol, and Japanese cultures. Koreans are justly very proud of this culture and heritage.

Korea is situated in the northeastern section of the Asian landmass (see map at the front of the book). The Korean peninsula hangs down from Manchuria, pointing in the direction of southern Japan. This central location has made it the scene of much of the history of the region; unfortunately, much of that history has been less than peaceful. Japan sees Korea as a "dagger pointed at the heart of Japan," with the frequent aggressor being China or its northern neighbor, Mongolia. As neither the Chinese nor the Mongolians (nor, for that matter, the Japanese) were particularly sea-faring peoples, Korea became the land bridge offering the most convenient route for invading armies from one direction or the other.   In the last two thousand years Korea has experienced roughly nine hundred invasions of various types and sizes; in more modern times invasion has visited the peninsula in

1592, 1597, 1627, and in the late Nineteenth and first half of the Twentieth Centuries. In addition, it has suffered through five major eras of foreign occupation — by China, the Mongols, Japan, the Soviet Union, and the United States (Oberdorfer, p. 3). The peninsula has too often seen itself destroyed by armies just trying to get to the throat of their more distant enemies, destroying everything in their path. The Korean perspective is that Korea is, to use its own phrase, "A shrimp among whales." Shrimp don't stay unscathed for long when whales are fighting around them, and Korea has been squashed between the thrashing tails of neighboring giants all too often in its history. Koreans have therefore understandably come to view their nation as the victim of larger, uncaring neighbors. Suspicion has grown to such an extent that even when neighbors reach out to help Korea in some of its periodic crises, there is an underlying feeling that the neighbor is only doing it for its own good. This has been true enough often enough that such suspicions are understandable, although frustrating to well-meaning helpers. In just the past century, Korea has been the site of international intrigue or warfare repeatedly:

1) during and after the Russo-Japanese War in 1904-05, which left Korea unwillingly in the growing Japanese sphere of influence;

2) between Japan and Korea during the Japanese colonial occupation of Korea from 1910 to 1945, during which systematic cultural destruction was carried out by the Japanese;

3) before and during World War II, when colonial Korea was used as a staging area and "behind the lines" storehouse of the Japanese. During this era Korea was forced to provide both male laborers for the Japanese war machine (particularly in mining) and female "Comfort Women" who were often girls just out of middle school, promised factory

15

jobs but ending up being forced to service the sexual needs of Japanese armies in the field under brutal conditions. These issues continue to erupt today, more than half a century after they occurred, due to a lack of an outright apology by Japan and insufficient or non-existent restitution. They continue to sour both international and sometimes interpersonal relations between Japanese and Koreans;

4) between June 1950 and July 1952, when the great powers of China and the United States (and allied U. N. forces) fought the first flare-up of the Cold War on the barren hills of Korea. No less then four times during the war was the capital, Seoul, won and lost, each time with terribly destructive consequences. Visitors to the skyscrapers and subways of Seoul today with its eleven million people can hardly imagine the Seoul of 1953, when the city was virtually flattened and its population reduced to about 100,000.

The catastrophes of 1) forty years of Japanese occupation, during which time the national culture and identity were nearly destroyed, 2) a brief and rocky period of military occupation by the United States in the South (1945-1948), 3) an even rockier period of struggling political forces during which the nation was sliced in half by outside forces (1948-1950), and 4) the culminating mass destruction and nearly total social chaos of the Korean War (1950-1952) created a society shaken to its very core culturally, physically, geographically, economically, and socially. Even eight years after the armistice, the South Korean society and economy were in shambles. In 1961 social disorder was still rampant. There were thousands upon thousands of war widows, over 100,000 orphans, and about 279,000 unemployed, of whom 72,000 were university graduates and 51,000 were discharged soldiers (*A Handbook of Korea, 1978*). The country was ripe for the revolution that occurred in April, 1961, when President

Rhee Sung-man (Syngman Rhee) was forced to step down. The Sixties and Seventies were years of the brutal dictatorship of General (later President) Park Chung-hee, who took the nation by the horns and tamed it into the beginnings of the economic powerhouse it was later to become. The price was that Korea became a police state dominated by strong military, with business and government connections and collusion often cemented by marriages. During this time travel outside of Korea was severely restricted, and for most people both economically and legally impossible. Park's assassination in 1979 resulted in the somewhat milder, but much more corrupt regime of President Chun Doo-hwan (who was the first Korean president to leave office peacefully at the end of his term). Chun was followed by a similarly corrupt (but much more mild-mannered) Roh Tae-woo (the first Korean president to take over for any length of time in a truly bloodless change of power). It has only been since the early 1990's that Korea has had any semblance of democracy. In that time former dissident Kim Young-sam became a viable presidential candidate and was elected, although only after joining the ruling party. Finally, in 1997 opposition leader and long-term democracy fighter Kim Dae-jung (no relation to the first Kim) was elected. This was the first time in Korean history that the ruling powers were ousted bloodlessly, honestly, and fairly in a true spirit of democracy. In February of 2003 Roh Moo-hyun, a former civil rights lawyer, took the presidency in a dramatic upset of the "old power" structure of old money and political ties.

Korea's economy has shown astronomic progress beginning with the autocratic, but forward-looking Park presidency in the early 1960s. During the Fifties and Sixties, and into the early Seventies, commodities were very scarce. U.S. government surplus food is still remembered by many middle aged Koreans today as a regular part of their school lunches in the 1960s (the steamed cornbread was particularly enjoyed; the American rice, not so much!) Let's take a look at some economic and social indicators of Korea during the years when the parents of the children in our classrooms were growing up.

- From 1949 to 2000 the South Korean population increased 230% from 20.2 to 47.6 million. (*Statistical Handbook of Korea, 2002*; www.nso.go.kr/handbook/eng)
- Between 1953 and 1997 the per capita income increased from US$67 to US$10,013. (*The Korea Herald* website, March 23, 2003) (dropped and recovered since then)
- Exports grew from US$22.3 million to US$150.4 billion between 1953 and 2001. (*Statistical Handbook of Korea, 2002*)
- In 1948 there were 12,294 registered vehicles (many ex-military); by 2003 this had increased more than a hundred-fold to 12,914,100, a decrease from roughly 1640 persons per vehicle to 3.7. (*Statistical Handbook of Korea, 2002*)
- Between 1948 and 2001 the number of elementary school children per teacher dropped from 57.8 to 28.7 (class size is larger than this). The literacy rate is 98%, with 90% completing high school and 14% completing college. (*Statistical Handbook of Korea, 2002*)
- In 1949 the number of people per doctor was 4615; by 2000 this had dropped to 648. (*Statistical Handbook of Korea, 2002*)
- South Korea has a life expectancy of 79 years for females; 72 for males (up from 59 and 66 years in 1971) (*Statistical Handbook of Korea, 2002*).

The Korea of the late Twentieth Century has experienced roughly two decades of sustained economic growth at a rate that is the envy of many more "developed" nations.

Thus, the economic collapse in Asia that began in the fall of 1997 in Korea took a tremendous toll on both Korean pride and the Korean pocketbook. As of this writing in the spring of 2003 there are strong signs that the nation and economy has emerged, after massive restructuring, stronger and certainly healthier than when it entered this stage. Certainly the nation is on the way "back up"; President Kim Dae-jung pronounced the economy "recovered" in December 1999, but there were still signs of unemployment beyond anything experienced in decades, and corporate restructuring and transparency were headline news into 2003.

Those familiar with the vibrant, exciting, technologically advanced, and economically aggressive Korea today can hardly believe that Korea was very much an underdeveloped country well into the 1960's, and a developing nation into the 1980's. During those decades hard work, "connections," a competitive spirit, and a good deal of luck were about the only ways to succeed or get ahead; of those who did succeed many sent their children overseas for an education, as Korean higher education was still limited in both quantity and quality. Many of our students' parents were such "education immigrants" who managed somehow to leave Korea during this era.

Traditional South Korean society has changed deeply in the last forty years. Since 1960 there has been a tremendous migration from the countryside to the city, with former peasants now working in urban factories. The capital city of Seoul alone, with a population of well over 11 million, has more than one-quarter of the nation's population. As farmers and fishermen of the Seventies sent their children to college, cities boomed as the countryside emptied of workers. As aging grandparents had to be cared for, many moved to the cities to be with children and grandchildren. Traditionally-minded, retired farmers living with their urbanized and much more Westernized children and grandchildren in small high-rise apartments in the city, and a rapid improvement in the standard of living, has created family and societal stress. Signs of this can be seen in some of the ethnic Korean children attending our schools.

It is important to understand this post-war history because this was the Korea in which the parents of our students grew up, and it shaped the way in which they look at themselves, at their children, and at the outside world. They are the products of a formerly devastated nation, poor in natural resources and overcrowded in population. They were raised at a time of such scarcity that those who did not fight to get ahead were left behind, whether in the economic race, in the education race, or in the race to catch the bus to work. Competition for education, for jobs, for housing, for transportation, and for places in the ranks of the successful was constant. Thus, while they were children and young adults, today's middle class developed a sense of fierce competition both with outsiders and among themselves, and may see themselves as being discriminated against by larger or more powerful neighbors. They grew up in a dictatorial police state in which individuals in power, and government in general, were obeyed but not highly respected.

Similarly, just as many adults in the West today were brought up by parents who grew up during the Depression but who themselves grew up in the economically healthy postwar years of the Fifties and Sixties, many of the ethnic Korea children we meet in our schools today are the children of an affluent Korea, but whose parents were brought up in the scraping poverty of a post-war nation devastated physically, economically, and socially. Today's parents, having experienced hardship themselves, may try to compensate by making sure that their children have whatever they need or want, particularly if it may in some way enhance their education or give them some advantage over their peers.

Forged in past centuries and more particularly in recent decades, a very strong sense of ethnic solidarity and family integrity has become part of the Korean psyche. This leads us to look next at the more traditional cultural aspects of their identity upon which this historical experience has been imposed.

TIME TO THINK . . .

How much do you know about the backgrounds of the parents of your students? Try to imagine the Korea in which they grew up. How might that background influence the way in which they raise their children?

How much do your ethnic Korean students know about the history of Korea? How might you work this into your curriculum, if appropriate?

How much are you a product of the period during which your parents were growing up? How has their childhood molded who you have become?

To learn more about the fascinating history of Korea, read *Korea's Place in the Sun*, by B. Cumings (see reference list).

CHAPTER III: CULTURAL BACKGROUND

Confucianism

Despite its recent and considerable social changes, South Korea is and has been, first and foremost, a very traditional nation based on the teachings of Confucius, who lived in China from 551 to 479 B. C. Unlike some other areas of East Asia, Confucianism as a religion is of minimal importance in Korea, but as a social system its influence touches each Korean from the moment of conception until death and even beyond. Korean culture and society are based on Confucian teachings, the goals of which are social harmony and stability based on the ideals of respect, duty, and loyalty towards older or more socially "superior" individuals and to members of one's extended family. This is accomplished through the recognition of four basic superior/inferior relationships among societal members: king/subject, father/child, husband/wife, and older brother/younger brother; and one lateral relationship: friend/friend. Confucianism as a philosophy and social system is infinitely more complicated than expressed on the chart on the next page, but for our purposes it will suffice. Confucian Korean society has a hierarchical structure in which the maintenance of harmonious and proper relationships is one of the highest of values. A critical aspect of these relationships is age: respect for older people by younger, and a balancing responsibility for younger by older. Respect and deference towards those in authority, be it the President, teacher, parents, older brother, older brother's friends, grandparents, or departed ancestors, is very much a part of the everyday life of Koreans. When two people meet for the first time, they immediately exchange their business cards, bow, and exclaim

22

FIVE BASIC CONFUCIAN
HEIRARCHICAL RELATIONSHIPS

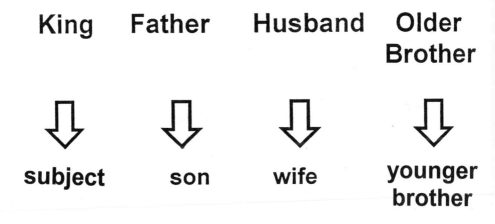

King	Father	Husband	Older Brother
⇩	⇩	⇩	⇩
subject	**son**	**wife**	**younger brother**

Friend ⇦⇨ Friend

(Adapted from *Handbook for Teaching Korean-American Students,* 1992)

silently but noticeably over the relative social position of the person (gleaned from the card) that they are meeting. Soon they have judged each other's respective status in the new relationship. This is of critical importance, as the Korean language has a number of "levels of respect" indicated by verb endings and in some cases, by vocabulary. A mistake in using too "low" a form towards someone of higher social status is taken very seriously, and has been the genesis for many a broken nose or fractured relationship. At a very young age Koreans learn how to judge the status of others and how to respond appropriately.

Within the family this superior/inferior relationship is taken even more seriously. Not only is great respect shown to parents, but to grandparents, older cousins, myriad aunts and uncles, and so on. On certain holidays and anniversaries of deaths special observances are held in the home or at gravesites to honor ancestors.

In school, both boys and girls fall into this environment of expected older/younger relationships, particularly among those of the same gender (and only within the Korean social group). Thus, a simple bow and the use of respectful language by younger students toward their "seniors" are often seen. Unfortunately, this is often enjoyed a little too much by the older students who might not want to recognize that they also have a reciprocal Confucian responsibility to take care of the younger students. If so, this may take the form of "teaching" the younger student(s) how to act towards them. Often, this is not a pretty scene, and frequently goes on unnoticed under unsuspecting Western eyes. Just as often, Korean parents wring their hands over it but just accept it as "the way things are."

Age and social superiority are also traditionally closely associated with wisdom. It stands to reason, then, that whatever grandfather would have done (or instructed) is most likely the right way to proceed. The old, traditional way has an intrinsic value if it was practiced by ancestors or is espoused by someone in authority (such as a teacher), especially in school or in the family. This, of course, can work against innovation or risk-taking of any kind, whether in school, business, or industry. Similarly (and we will explore this in more detail later) we see that in schools the teacher, as a parent/authority figure, is very highly respected; thus, the word of the teacher is taken very seriously and is not questioned, at least in front of the teacher.

This strong deference to authority and superiors is the root of both Korea's impressive social stability and many of its frequent tragedies and ills. All too often, those in positions of inferior status don't speak up when they need to, fearing reprisal or risking insult to a superior on whom they later may have to depend. A tragic example of this is suggested by the March 28, 1998 *Korea Herald* story found below, regarding the crash of a Korean Air 747 while approaching the airport in Guam on August 6, 1997. (The highlighting of a critical passage did not appear in the original article.)

Cultural factors on trial at Korean Air crash inquiry

HONOLULU, Hawaii (AFP) — Indications that cultural factors may have played a role in the Korean Air crash in Guam last year are emerging from the investigation of the disaster which left 228 people dead.

Evidence of confusion in the cockpit of the Boeing 747 and the crew's failure to react to warning signs has confounded investigators after two days of hearing into the disaster here.

The jumbo jet plowed into a hillside some five km (three

25

miles) short of the runway after the plane had descended below minimum altitudes.

By the time the captain reacted, the plane was going too fast toward the ground to be saved, investigators say.

They have noted concern that traditional respect for age and seniority in South Korea may prevent junior officers from speaking up in the cockpit.

Captain Lee Jung-taek, chief of flight crew operations for the airline, testifying Wednesday, denied this was so. But he said that in the months after the crash, Korean Air has strengthened its training to give junior officers more authority in the cockpit.

On the first day of the hearing called by the National Transportation Safety Board Tuesday, the cockpit voice recorder was played, covering the last 30 minutes of the plane's flight on August 6, 1997.

Certainly the Guam crash was a particularly tragic example of ancient Confucianism running headlong into modern technology. However, it is safe to say that business, politics, education, and any aspect of Korean society is affected in both positive and negative ways by the respect shown elders or those higher in rank.

On the positive side, respect for others in authority is what makes the city of Seoul, with 11 million people, a place where one can walk the streets at night without fear. Only in recent years has there been talk of teenage delinquency, and one rape or murder by a single teen makes the front pages and causes Koreans to search their collective souls for what went wrong with their society. A similar crime in Los Angeles or New York would hardly make the first section of the paper. Koreans are remarkably traditional, following time-honored rules of conduct (if not always respecting particular laws, especially those related to traffic). This aspect of their culture makes it all the more difficult to survive in a society with one hand on an ox-drawn plow and the other clutching a cell phone.

RELATIONSHIPS:
Maintaining Harmony and Balance

It is not just important to build and retain relationships in Korea; building *harmonious* relationships among peers or family members is critical. Unfortunately, this emphasis on harmony conflicts all too often with the Western, individualistic forces that face its people today, especially when they live outside of Korea or work in multicultural environments in Korea. Balancing this emphasis on harmony is the recognition that opposites balance each other. That these concepts are well represented by the flag of the Republic of Korea, shown on the next page, is no accident. The circle in the center represents harmony and unity. Movement and fluidity are seen in the "um/yang" ("yin/yang" in Chinese) circle. Within this circle the two halves symbolize opposing but synergetic opposites (male/female, good/evil, life/death, etc.) Thus, the unity of life and the universe is complete with even opposites contributing. The four sets of corner bars seen in the flag, called *kwae*, further support this idea of opposites, representing heaven/south; earth/north; sun/east; and moon/west.

Because Korean thought is so imbued with this basic idea of balancing opposites, situations demanding shades of gray, moderation, and relativity are difficult to understand and even communicate in the Korean language. Ideas like "biculturalism" or "mixed race" are anathema, either not understood or simply considered not "pure." Korean society

SOUTH KOREAN FLAG, The "Tae-guk-ki"

has been monocultural and conservative for so long, with one traditional "right" way to do things that anything from outside or which may be different is seen as a threat. It is a testament to Korean practicality that despite these values, the nation has changed so dramatically in so many ways in the past forty years, although not without tremendous social cost. As a result of the high value placed on doing things the "Korean way," diversity and differences are often considered to be negative. Homogeneity and conformity are valued; individuality and free thinking have negative value. The Asian proverb, "The nail that sticks up gets pounded down" applies to Korea, as well. The Korean emphasis on the past, on respect for authority and learning, on loyalty to the family or nation, and on conformity to the standards set by the group have worked against creativity and free thinking. These also place tremendous pressures on ethnic Koreans living outside of Korea. While conformity is important, they face the question of

As a result of the high value placed on doing things the "Korean way," diversity and differences are often considered to be negative.

with whom they should conform — those of the nation in which they live? Those in the international community? Fellow Koreans? Unless they live in a Korean community overseas, they may find themselves nonconformists in their new environment. Conforming to the values of their new home, however, may imply disloyalty or dissatisfaction with the older Korean way and may make later re-entry to Korea very difficult, not to mention causing conflict with more traditional parents and grandparents. This dilemma will be discussed further in Chapter V.

Let's look at how the idea of maintaining harmony plays out in every day social interactions. Certainly the primary expression of this is the real hesitancy among Koreans to openly disagree with one another, especially within a social group, which would upset the good feelings and harmony. A person who disagrees with some-

"The nail that sticks up gets pounded down."

one he considers his "senior" quite often just says nothing (a phenomenon not unknown in the West!). Often the superior may express his or her opinion and everyone compliantly nods their heads, no individual being willing to speak up. One should also not say things that may make others feel bad, or refuse to go along with the group activity. As group drinking among men is very common, and getting drunk seems to be the aim, all too often a person who really doesn't want to join in goes along due to strong peer pressure. We are not talking about teenagers, but about adult professionals. To say, "Just a coke, please" and not share the common and all too frequently filled cup is to upset the harmony and sense of "group-ness." This tendency to keep things on an even keel also often results in people keeping bad news from one another until the last possible moment. This can wreak havoc with international families, in which dad might not be told until late in the game that he is being transferred. He might in turn keep it from mom for a while, unless of course she is anxious to go home. Together they may keep the news from the children until the very last minute so that their sadness at leaving friends won't upset their studies. Bad news is often kept from superiors, as well. It is very possible, for example, that Kim Young Sam, president during the economic collapse in late 1997, was not told of the full extent of the precariousness of the economy by his subordinates until it was too late to do anything because no one wanted to be the bearer of bad news.

The net result of this emphasis on harmony and peacefulness is a nation in which bad news is often covered up or ignored until too late; it is a nation of people wearing masks. Koreans often criticize foreigners for being too open with emotions, be it happiness or anger. Korean girls are taught to cover their mouths when they laugh. Loud laughter is frowned upon; similarly anger is held in check. (One time that emotions *are* very evident is at funerals, when wailing, crying, and moaning are expected. Traditionally, a rich family may even have hired paid "wailers" to cry in their place.)

Related to this idea is the tendency to save dignity and "face," both one's own and that of others. Seldom does one want to make another look bad, and even more important is the desire to never bring any kind of shame on one's family. Public apologies are rare; it is expected that everyone would "understand" that one did wrong and is of course sorry – that in itself is considered shame and apology enough.

Consistent with the idea of maintaining harmony is the emphasis on group loyalty and membership; group members at work, school, church, or at home are expected to "go along to get along." A well known and oft quoted Korean proverb states "The bamboo bends, the stick breaks." This is, if you are rigid and cling too closely to your position, you will be broken. However, if like the bamboo you bend in the wind and give in, you will survive to live and bend another day. Perhaps, one day you will survive to be the biggest bamboo, and everyone else will bend in the direction you are leaning. Thus, it is important to remember in working with Korean parents that apparent agreement does not necessarily mean compliance. You may never know what Mrs. Kim is really thinking, despite the fact that she smiles, nods, and says, "Yes, yes." More on that later.

"The bamboo bends, the stick breaks."

An important aspect of maintaining harmony is the recognition of the hierarchical system of social relationships discussed earlier. As long as each individual knows his or her place, stays in that place, and pays proper respect to those above, harmony results. When a person upsets the status quo by not recognizing proper etiquette, by humiliating another, or by causing unnecessary conflict, relationships become unbalanced and disharmony results.

RELATIONSHIPS: Home and Family

The importance of the family cannot be underestimated in a Confucian society. It is the basic building block of the nation. One's allegiance is first to the family; it is no accident of language that in Korean the family name comes first. When a person gives his name, he or she is first identifying from what family he or she comes (traceable back to a particular village and a particular ancestor over many hundreds of years through genealogies still in print); the next two syllables of the name are the generational and individual names.

It is important to remember that "family" always means the extended family of grandparents, uncles and aunts, and cousins, particularly on the paternal side. It may seem harsh and cruel to a Westerner that Korean parents might leave a child behind with relatives in Korea during an overseas move; this seems perfectly logical and normal for a Korean. The parting will of course hurt, but at least the child is with family. A childless older brother often becomes the legal and practical parent of a child of a younger brother who has more than his share of sons. The child may never know that "father" is really "uncle"; on the other hand, it is not that important — family is family. Although adoptions are very infrequent among Koreans (except within a family), when they do happen they are occasions for sadness and pity. More often than not, the child is never told that he or she is adopted. To do so would make the child feel that he or she has no family, as they in fact are not part of the adoptive family's bloodline. Koreans have a very difficult time understanding, and are truly in awe of Western families, who can adopt a Korean child as their own and love this child who looks so different and does not share a bloodline like "one of the family."

Family support and nurture extends far beyond childhood. Even when going off to another city to college, it is common for a young person to live with a relative. No thought is given to paying for expenses; it's all in the family. Young women in particular are protected and are often expected to live at home during college and until marriage. Today, choice of a mate is wider than ever, but still about half of all marriages are partly arranged by parents who set up "meetings" between their adult child and an eligible (and acceptable) partner from the family of a parental friend or co-worker. Normally young people are given "veto" over these attempts by parents to find a good mate, although the pressure can be high when there are younger siblings waiting for an older brother or sister to get married so they can marry in turn. It must be understood that a young woman is not just marrying a young man; she is marrying into a new family. She becomes a member of her husband's extended family, and the connection between her family and his family is now cemented and may have future commercial or other benefits for both families (similar to European royal matches of the past). It is still very common to read in the newspaper that a rich young woman from a family with a tradition of service in government or politics has been married to an even richer young man whose family is deeply involved with business or high finance. Not only is the *couple* married; the *families* are married, and everyone benefits, or may soon do so.

After marriage, a young woman joins her husband's family, possibly moving in with parents-in-law, especially if the husband is an oldest son. Should the new couple need a car, or apartment, or money to start a business, the husband's parents would often expect to provide these if they could. Letting a new couple "suffer it out" for a year or two before they get on their feet is not considered good practice. Even married, professional sons in their thirties and forties are often the recipients of an apartment from parents. While this may seem like a case of extended apron strings, the apartment does not really belong to the couple, it belongs to the extended family, and is an investment in the family's future.

33

A young couple never really "sets out on their own" but rather becomes a new segment of the husband's extended family.

It is true that in the traditional Confucian family, the oldest male truly rules the roost. His word is law, and he is both revered and feared. However, the traditional Western image of the Oriental wife dutifully following twelve steps behind her husband is only half the truth. While in public, the wife will most often take a very subservient, servant-like pose. In the home, however, the wife is both influential and strong. It is no accident that in Korean, one of the words for "wife" literally means "inside person;" that for "husband" means "outside person." This does not refer to washing the dishes or cutting the grass; rather, it indicates that the husband is the family's "front" to the world, and the one who goes *out* to bring home the income. Conversely, the wife is in control of much of what goes on within the home, and is not afraid to take responsibility for those areas. Two areas in which women are particularly influential within the walls of the home are finances and the raising of children, including their education.

Most often, when a Korean husband comes home on payday with his briefcase of cash (or today, when the money is transferred automatically on-line into the family bank account from the place of employment) he hands it over to his wife. She then gives him his spending money. She is both the chief financial officer and holder of the keys in the family. If the couple lives with parents-in-law, the son often hands his salary over to his mother (as female head of the house) instead of to his wife. Mom who would give him his personal monthly "allowance."

The wife may make real estate decisions, invest money, or lend to or borrow money from friends or relatives, sometimes without the husband's agreement or even knowledge. More than one marriage has broken up (behind closed doors) when the wife lent money to a friend to whom she could not say "no" (because of the relationship), and the money was lost. Husbands are often guilty of this, as well. Groups of women often pool their money in what are called "kye" so that one or another has enough at one time to marry off a daughter, buy a new apartment, or make an investment. Unfortunately for the wife in an overseas situation, she may find herself without any purse strings to control. She may not be able to speak the local language and may have no money in a local bank. She may be dependent upon her husband or a local national in the company office to help her in this area. This may rob her of a very important tool of real power in the family, and may cause her no small amount of insecurity.

The other area for which the Korean wife has almost total control and responsibility is that of the raising of the children, including supervising their education. As we shall see later on, education is a harsh experience for Korean children. From the time they enter elementary school until the time they graduate from high school, they are in a rigid, unforgiving, highly competitive, and sometimes cruel system. They must study grueling hours and compete relentlessly against others who may be more talented. Korean moms provide the discipline to make this happen.

Possibly to compensate for the rigor of school life ahead in middle and high school, small children are often indulged outside of school. Discipline is often very lax by Western standards, whether it be in a restaurant or even at a wedding, where they are allowed to wander around at will. They seldom have a set bedtime; toys, candy, and money are often given out freely. Boys are especially spoiled in this way, particularly if they are oldest sons. They are waited on

The other area for which the Korean wife has almost total control and responsibility is that of the raising of the children, including supervising their education.

at home and may expect the same treatment in school. In Korea, it is a common opinion among young women that they should not marry an oldest son because they don't make very responsible husbands (and few want to live with an overbearing mother-in-law who will often very soon begin demanding a grandson!) Children seldom have chores or responsibilities at home; they are to devote themselves to their studies.

On the other hand, discipline can be both terrible and swift, with a firm spanking being given when a mother finally tires of a whining child. For older children, getting hit across the palm of the hands with a bamboo stick or ruler, being hit across the back of the calves with a good sized stick (even at school), being sent out of the house to sleep on the doorstep, or getting the "silent treatment" from parents for a few days is not unusual. Actual bruises are rare, but certainly not unknown. Korean discipline for both children and adults is based on shame rather than on guilt; therefore anything that makes the child feel ashamed, even publicly, meets its purpose. International educators are placed in a difficult positions when a child has done something that must be reported to the parents, knowing full well that as a result the child may receive a form of discipline at home that is outside the acceptability range of the Westerner.

A Korean mom often takes responsibility for her children's shortcomings and mistakes. If a child gets in trouble in school the mother will acknowledge that the child did wrong, but then in the child's presence may say that the child should not be punished because actually it was the mother's fault (sometimes the father will say this about the mother, too!) She was too lenient, she didn't teach the child properly, etc., etc., but now the child knows better, and needn't be disciplined at school. Being faced with a parent who is pleading not to discipline a child can present a challenge for school authorities who are trying to maintain a consistent discipline policy. (Parents are often particularly worried that the incident will be noted in the child's permanent file, as it would be in Korean school, and that this may affect future educational plans.)

Many Korean parents desperately want their children to "fit in" with the important peer group. The need to be part of the group, to not be seen as strange or different, is very, very important. Korean children are not unlike children elsewhere in using this as a way to get what they want. Requests for a phone in the room, a particular cell phone, a certain brand of jeans or backpack, etc., etc., do not fall of deaf ears at home. If "everyone else has one" and your child doesn't, your child may not fit in properly. The group solidarity may be disrupted, and certainly your child may end up as an outsider rather than as a safe group member. This would reflect poorly on both the child and the family.

Children are at the bottom of the Confucian hierarchy, and are certainly to be seen and not heard. Alternately spoiled and disciplined, possibly it is only Confucian respect for parents that keeps the children from rebelling. They are usually really nice kids!

KOREAN NAMES

Korean names are generally composed of three syllables: a family name followed by a two-syllable given name. (Remember, then, to always ask for "fa mily" and "individual" names rather than "last" or "first" names on school forms!) Sometimes, one of the two syllables of the given name is a generational name shared by all children (particularly boys) of that generation in that extended family. These syllables are determined for generations in the future. Thus, two Shin brothers may be named Shin Byong-kyu and Shin Wang-kyu, sharing the syllable "ky u." Their male cousins on their father's side would most likely also share that syllable if the family were keeping with tradition. A married woman keeps her own family name, only changing it informally to "Mrs. Soon-hee Park" (wife of Mr. Park) for the benefit of foreigners who may be confused if they are told that her real name is "Kwon, Soon-hee." Other women may choose not to change, particularly if they are professionals in their own right. Therefore, the fact that Mr. Park is married to Miss (or Ms. or Mrs.) Kwon does in no way indicate a blended family. Additionally confusing is that within the Korean community parents are often known simply as "Su ng-ho's mom" or "Myong-ji n's dad." A child's family name always follows the father's, as he or she is considered to be a member of that family. Further making Korean names difficult for Westerners (or maybe easier?) is the fact that there are very few family names, fewer than 250 altogether. The most common are "Kim" (Kimm, Ghim), "Park" (Pahk, Park, Bak, Bahk, etc.) and Yi (actually "E e," but usually spelled and pronounced "Lee" outside of Korea). A few others such as "Choi" (Che, Cheh, Chey), "Ch ung," "Cho," "Shin," " Yoo," and "Han " make up the lion's share of the remainder.

    A Korean's given name is very personal property, and is not something to be thrown around carelessly. Only children are called by their given names; the author, after working closely with his secretary for more than 15 years, still calls her "Mrs. Woo" (Actually, "Woo" is her husband's family name that she uses only professionally. Outside of the Western school community, she is still goes by her original family name of Hwang). Adults are never called by their given names except by older family members or close childhood friends.

In public, Koreans are most often called by their professional title or the catchall, "son-s aeng," which literally means "teacher, " often with the honorific " nim" added at the end. Thus, a person would be called "Doctor ," "Pastor," "Director," "Principal," "Pilot," etc., with or without a family name preceding it. Brothers or sisters (and even friends of the same generation) would call each other "brothe r" or "sister." Adult graduates of the same high school may call each other "sonbae" or "hubae" depending on whether they are older or younger than the person addressed.

What's the safest thing for a Westerner to do? Simply call children by their given name, and call adults by the Western style "Mr." "Miss," or " Mrs." followed by their family name (When in doubt, use the family name of their children. Don't worry, you'll be forgiven if you make a mistake!)

RELATIONSHIPS: Classmates and Peers

After a child has learned the rudiments of Confucian relationships at home, he or she is ready to branch out into the world of peer relationships. It was mentioned earlier that older/younger relationships are learned early in life. They are to be developed for security here and now, regardless of age. Lateral friend/friend relationships, however, are developed for both the present and the future. Korean children, particularly in high school and in college, consciously build relationships to last a lifetime. The importance of building relationships deep in quality and with the right kind of people from the right families is crucial to one's future. The importance of peers (and peer pressure) is much more than a passing adolescent need; it extends into adulthood. High school classmates may call on each other for social or economic favors or help decades into adulthood, whether it be to get a building

39

permit or for a sizable private loan. In addition, a young person who attends a particular university may well spend much of his or her professional life working with fellow alumni, as many of the larger Korean companies hire primarily graduates of a particular university, often the alma mater of the founder of the company. Even in education this holds true. Today nearly 95% of Seoul National University professors are graduates of that school; this type of inbreeding is not uncommon. Many of those in positions of power and influence during the Park Chung-hee, Chun Doo-hwan, and Roh Tae-woo regimes had been classmates of these leaders decades before at the Korea Military Academy. (In an interesting twist of fate, Park Chung-hee's classmate from the second postwar class of the ROK army officers' training course was a man named Kim Jae-kyu, who was not only Park's chief of the many-tentacled Korean CIA, but was also Park's eventual assassin. In this case apparently the old school tie wore too thin.) It is no coincidence that favors were passed out and money changed hands at such a rate during the presidencies of Chun and Roh that both men and many of their classmates spent time in jail following their leaving office.

While the web of relationships gives Korean society a good deal of its resiliency, it also is the root of many of its weaknesses. In a system in which the maintenance of relationships ranks near the top in social values, in which the rule of law has traditionally not been respected (at least behind closed doors), and in which any small advantage can make the difference between success and failure for one and one's family, graft and corruption eat away at the core of society. Favors are cemented with gifts; good deeds are not forgotten by either party. "Winking" at the rules by government officials to help an old friend or even a friend of a friend, acknowledged by an envelope of cash or promise of future favors, has resulted in more than one bridge or building collapse, and once exposed has cut short the tenure of more than one cabinet minister. Ongoing political scandal is a fact of life in South Korea today, even as the nation struggles to don new garments of democracy and open government. Democracy has taken firm root in South Korea, but graft and corruption are endemic in society, government, and business. This unfortunate phenomenon was summed up by a Korean political science professor at Sook Myung University amid widespread public cries for clean government in January 2000. "We understand that we can't survive or compete in international society as long as our system is based on corruption and bribery. But it's something like air for Koreans. It's very difficult to eradicate." (*The Korea Herald*, p. 11, January 25, 2000). Fortunately, most Korean individuals do not reflect this darker side of Confucianism.

RELATIONSHIPS: Within Social Groups

As noted earlier, the importance of membership in a group rather than standing alone as an individual cannot be underestimated. Beyond the family and smaller peer group, Koreans are closely identified by the larger groups to which they belong. Once a relationship is established between an individual and other members of a group, it is very difficult and painful to break. Normally, when an individual is mentioned in the newspaper (whether it be complimentary or not) he or she is mentioned as a member of a particular company. If a young person gets in trouble, the police immediately call the school, rather than the home, and the newspaper will report that "Park, second year student at "X" High School, whose father is a salary worker at "Y" Company . . . ." Companies pride themselves on the "family" atmosphere they create among their employees. Traditionally, employment is for life, and the Korean economic disaster of the late 1990's that resulted in forced closings and layoffs was much more emotionally traumatic than it would have been in the West. In addition to the obvious loss of income for the laid-off employee, the idea of being expelled from the group that has been a source of both economic security and personal identity is sometimes fatal. More than one father and husband has committed suicide or pretended to go to work for months rather than admit to his wife and children that he no longer has a job, so much is one's identity tied to the company. Changing companies in mid-career is both unusual and suspect. Only since the mid 1990s, with large numbers of men who worked for very respectable companies out in the street after a corporate collapse, has this become more socially acceptable.

One group that most international schools must acknowledge is the "Korean moms' group." These informal groups exist for mutual support in an unfamiliar educational environment. Each has its own hierarchy (based on comparative ages, colleges of graduation, or husbands' positions). The groups usually work quite well in terms of support, but they can sometimes become so exclusive that certain women are not allowed in, sometimes on the basis of their children's comparative school success (or rather, lack thereof). In addition, while such groups can be used by the school to "get the word out" on particular issues and in communicating the school's mission, they can also be destructive if misinformation is disseminated as truth by someone higher up in the social strata. It would take a strong woman to disagree or act not in accordance with the feelings of the group or its leader.

For children and young people in any culture, being accepted by friends is certainly important, especially as middle and high school students grow away from family and associate more with peers. For a Korean child, not to be accepted by the group is doubly difficult. Mothers will work very hard to be sure that their child is not left out, whether this means buying the jacket, shoes, or book bag "style of the month" or giving large amounts of money to kids so they can take friends out to eat. The child who is consciously ostracized by other students is in serious trouble. Kids who are picked on, called names, become targets for lunch money "loans," or find themselves purposely left out of games or other social events are called *"wahng-tah."* These children are frequent suicides in Korea. Parents and society recognize this social problem but seem helpless to do much about it. Both parents and students are fearful of reprisal and seldom speak up against this type of bullying and abuse (much as many American parents recognize the dangers of available street drugs, but are afraid to speak up for fear of reprisal and hope that somehow their child is immune). Many a TV documentary has highlighted this serious societal problem. As with bullies around the world, today's *"wahng-tah"* too often becomes tomorrow's bully. The child (or adult) with no friends is more than just a "loner" in Korea; he or she is to be pitied above all others.

One group that most international schools must acknowledge is the "Korean moms' group."

College freshmen are often "initiated" into their new group by upper classmen and even by professors with nights of heavy drinking similar to some fraternity or sorority initiations in the United States. This tragically results annually in deaths by alcohol poisoning at the beginning of the academic year.

Wh ether it be the family, the social group, the church, the company, the club, or the graduating class, Koreans seek out groups with which to identify to a degree most Westerners would think unhealthy. Subservience of one's own needs to those of the group, following the group's leaders, or following an undesired career path for the sake of the family are common themes in Korean society.

RELATIONSHIPS: With the Korean Nation

A Korean's relationship with his or her nation is also very deep and sacred. The pride of Koreans for Korea is the basis for many of the very positive qualities found in the country, as well as for some of the difficulties it faces when coming into contact with other nations. During the 1960's students were actually taught in school that after Germans, Koreans were the smartest "race" in the world! The fact that Koreans are very homogenous physically, that they have lived on a small peninsula for 5000 years together, that their written language was developed specifically for use with their spoken language and is used no place else in the world (except by expatriate Koreans), and finally that they have repeatedly been victims of hostile outside forces, has forged them into a proud, loyal, and solid people. This feeling of collective nationhood well expressed in the language; in Korean it is very awkward to say "My nation" as might be said in many other languages — it is always expressed "Uri nara" – "*Our* nation." (The solidity of the family unit is also demonstrated in this way; one always says "*our* family" rather than "*my* family.") This strong sense of "*we* Koreans" and "everyone else" is also apparent in the Korean word for "foreigners," which literally means "outside people." Koreans who emigrate from Korea are always thought of as "overseas Koreans" rather than as Canadians or British of Korean descent. When an overseas Korean of another citizenship becomes famous in politics or sports, he or she is considered by Koreans to be "really one of us." Bloodlines run deep: Koreans generally consider ethnicity rather than citizenship to be the basis of determining nationality. One interesting example of this occurred a few years ago when a U.S. citizen of Korean background rose quite high in the U.S. intelligence establishment. He came into contact with classified material (concerning Korea) that he illegally passed on to the Korean government. In explaining his behavior, he readily admitted that he had been spying. However, he excused himself by saying that there was no reason for the U.S. to keep the information from an ally, Korea, and therefore he was justified to pass it on to his "motherland." He failed to recognize that as a U.S. citizen he was no longer a Korean, and that his loyalties had to lie with the United States, not Korea. The Korean press roundly supported him in this, saying that he really had a duty to help his motherland rather than the United States, which should have given the information to Korea, anyway. Most Koreans, having a very difficult time separating the man's U.S. nationality from his Korean ethnicity, thought he was completely justified in what he had done. Interestingly, the Korean government steered clear of this entire incident, citing it as an "internal U.S. matter."

Another example of this strong connection with Korea is the comment made on U.S. television by an ethnic Korean

Chicago shopkeeper during the Rodney King riots in Los Angeles in the spring of 1992: "If my family lives in America for five generations, we will still be Korean!" We can hardly imagine a first generation German or Polish American saying such a thing.

This characteristic of identification as a Korean and as a member of the Korean nation forever is an important point to consider in understanding our students. Firstly, it explains some of their tendency to stick together reported by educators in many schools. Secondly, it works to their detriment when and if they return to Korea, when they become "hidden immigrants" in a homogeneous nation. (see Pollock and Van Reken). Although they look Korean on the outside, they are exposed as pseudo-Koreans as soon as they speak another language. Ethnic Koreans who speak other languages in public in Korea are often ostracized. "Are you Korean or not?" is less a question than a rhetorical "What's *wrong* with you?" Children who have lived overseas are criticized by their grandparents for not speaking, bowing, or behaving properly, and a good deal of identity struggle results. On one hand they are told not to forget that they are Koreans, and on the other that they are not very good ones. This will be discussed in greater depth later.

> *"If my family lives in America for five generations, we will still be Korean!"*

CONCLUSION

The preceding section has described the foundations of Korean culture. It would be incorrect to give the reader the impression that every Korean child or adult behaves in the ways described. During the past twenty years Korea has undergone tremendous changes. The firm Confucian base has been under attack by Western culture and values. The importance of family and of social harmony and stability have been shaken by an invasion of Western ideas such as individual rights, children's rights, and the rights of women. A culture which has traditionally been based on respect to the oldest has given way to one filled with commercialism aimed at the "under thirty" generation. As people have traveled outside of Korea, particularly young people, they have seen that there are different ways of living and acting which are both frightening and attractive. The nation has gone from being a primarily agrarian society to one that is urban based, and the tools of survival (and technological output) have changed in one generation from ox-drawn plows and strong backs to cell phones and laptops. The Korean parents and children we see in our international schools today are in the vanguard of that change, but beneath the cosmopolitan surface the core characteristics discussed above are alive and well. Therein lies the struggle of our students' parents. They are products of a very traditional society, the traditions of which are at the core of their identity. At the same time they are trying to balance that traditionalism with an international lifestyle and the knowledge that the longer they are away from Korea, the less their children will be "Korean." Conflict results from wanting their children to have the benefits of a Western education while not falling prey to the uglier sides of Western culture. This conflict is seen most vividly in our Western-style schools.

In the next section we shall look at Korean education, examine the childhood educational experiences of our students' parents, try to understand their view of education, discuss why Korean education has evolved the way it has, and see how it both conflicts with and supports the goals of our Western style schools.

TIME TO THINK . . .

Think about some of your ethnic Korean students. What characteristics mentioned in this section have you seen in them? Which seem totally foreign to what you have observed?

Ask yourself the same questions about the parents of your students. Are you beginning to understand them a little better? What questions do you still have? Jot them down and think about them as you read the next section.

How strong is your own sense of personal ethnic identity? To what extent does it define you? To what extent is it irrelevant?

What are the basic values of your culture? If you are from a Jewish or Christian background, how has your religious background affected your core Western values? How might the values of your religion conflict with your culture? If you are not of a Jewish or Christian background, how have the teachings of these religions affected your culture, and in turn your personal values? How much are we products of our national cultures, and how much products of our chosen religion?

CHAPTER IV: EDUCATION

The One Right Answer

Formal education in Korea dates back to the Koguryo kingdom's *Taehak* state schools, established in 372 A.D., which provided select young men from the upper classes with an academic and military education in preparation for careers in the government or military. Korea continued to have a strong tradition of education up to and throughout the Yi Dynasty (1392-1910 A.D.), albeit mainly for the male gentry. Traditionally, the hardworking sons of farmers and fishermen, even if they had the inclination and ability to study, had little time for such non-productive work. Thus, educated people traditionally were almost totally from the upper social classes. Consequently teachers, as holders of knowledge, came to be associated with social superiority and high status. The honorific Korean word for any adult, *"sunsaeng-nim,"* literally means "teacher." This respect accorded teachers is still alive today and is one reason Korean children are often such a joy to teach.

This system stayed in place until the arrival in 1910 of the Japanese, who imposed an educational system that was, although designed to keep Koreans in a low social, economic, and political status, at least not limited to only the gentry. The traditional influence, though, is still found in every classroom in Korea today.

The teacher/student relationship, like all else in Korean society, takes on Confucian overtones. The teacher is considered by both the child and society to be fulfilling very much a parental role. The diagram on the next page illustrates this.

TEACHER
(parent/father figure)

| KNOWLEDGE | OBEDIENCE |
| WISDOM | RESPECT |

STUDENT
(child/son figure)

CONFUCIAN STUDENT/TEACHER
RELATIONSHIP

This traditional Confucian education for the elite consisted primarily of memorizing many thousands of Chinese characters and the five Confucian classics. Unfortunately, Chinese characters are learned only one way — by memorization. There is no alphabet, although there are simple "radicals" with particular meanings that together may be used to build larger characters. There is little room for creativity; *there is but one right way* to write a particular character. For the student, the teacher's word was law: for generations these characters had been written with each of the various strokes of a given character written in a particular order; to write them otherwise would reflect poorly on ancestors and great scholars who came before. As an example, take a look on the next page at the two characters that make up the word "Han-kuk," the South Korean word for "Korea." The first character, *"Han,"* literally means "Korea." It is made of eighteen strokes, each written in order, as seen in the diagram. The second character, *"Kuk,"* means "nation." It has no less than twelve strokes. Thus, to write one word, "Korea," a student must learn thirty strokes, each in proportion to the other, in a particular order, each with little meaning and no single sound associated with it.

Given that a South Korean high school graduate today must learn roughly 1,800 characters just to be able to read the newspaper, it is obvious that a great deal of time must be spent in memorization. Interestingly, Korea has its own excellent phonetic alphabet of 28 letters called *Hangul*, developed under the direction of King Sejong in 1433 A.D. For hundreds of years, however, the upper classes kept this simple and logical system from the masses, thus maintaining their monopoly on learning and power. Later on the Japanese outlawed the use of this system in their unsuccessful step-by-step effort to eradicate Korean culture and replace it with Japanese. Only since the Japanese departure in 1945 has *Hangul* been in widespread use, and it is rightfully a source of great pride to Koreans. In formal documents and in the newspaper, it is often still mixed with Chinese characters to clarify the meaning of Korean homonyms. Interestingly, in North Korea *Hangul* is used almost exclusively without the mixing of Chinese characters still evident in the South.

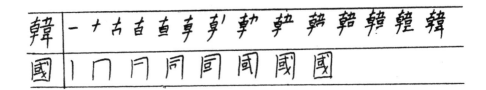

CHINESE CHARACTERS FOR "HANKUK"

"Hankuk," the name of South Korea, requires a total of 30 strokes, each memorized and written in order.
(Characters by Soon-ok Borden)

Although towards the end of the Nineteenth Century Christian missionaries set up some Western-style schools for children from all social classes, recruiting some literally off the streets, because of widespread fear of foreigners these did not receive much support among the upper classes despite the encouragement of the forward-looking Queen Min. After liberation from Japan in 1945 and the U.S. military occupation in 1948, an educational system based on the Japanese model was re-adopted as it conformed to both Confucian ethics and the traditional Korean style of instruction.

Korean education today is little different in philosophy and methodology than it was in the 1960's, when the parents of our students went to school. Now, as then, memorization is the chief mode of transferring knowledge and information from the learned teacher to the ignorant child. Long after education stopped consisting almost solely of the memorization of Chinese characters the methodology of lecture and memorization is still firmly in place. Large class sizes (today still more than fifty students per class in urban areas; fewer in rural areas) also lend themselves to lecture rather than discussion. Campaigns to integrate foreign language (primarily English) conversation and discussion classes, for example, fall flat in classes of fifty students in which the teacher wishes to maintain complete control. Similarly, constant public discussion about encouraging creativity, fostering thinking skills, encouraging inquiry, or rewarding initiative by students faces an uphill battle in a system that has long valued and promoted a "one right answer" ethos originally based on the "one right way" to memorize a character or a Chinese classic. Learning the right answers and agreeing with the teacher or with older students are valued characteristics. If the teacher, the book's author, the older student, or a parent or grandparent states that an answer is correct, then there is no more argument. There can only be one "right" answer. Lively discussion, creative thinking, alternative solutions, and intellectual independence are neither welcome in the classrooms of Korea at any level nor are they conducive to earning high grades or respect from the teacher. To conform, to harmonize, and to accept the status quo spells success in the Korean educational system.

The Korean educational community is constantly working to adopt more Western methodologies and aims, but the inertia of the traditional educational establishment is strong. Constant attempts at educational reform by the national Ministry of Education, where educational policy is set, have met with frustration and resistance, even from teachers. Top down decisions have met serious resistance from below while militant teacher organizations put the blame for sluggish reform on the Ministry of Education above. It is interesting that even as Korea looks to the West for guidance in this area, the West (particularly the United States) looks with envy on education in countries like Korea and Japan, which appear to have such an effective system. The truth is that Korean education shines where memorization and "one right answer" styles of teaching and learning are most appropriate: in mathematics. Korean students do well in many other areas, but their excellence is based mostly on recall rather than deeper understanding. Writing skills are often weak, as are thinking skills. Creativity is shunned; critical thinking is not rewarded. On the other hand, musical ability is often strong. Could this be because in order to truly excel in music a student needs to practice, practice, practice? Certainly the Korean educational style would foster strength in such an area.

Adherence to such a system is also encouraged by the fact that college entrance rests almost solely on standardized exams. Students' outside interests, talents, or abilities are simply not considered in the process of evaluation; success on these college entrance exams rests on memorization of the right answers for the test questions. Thus, the entire educational establishment, especially at the high school level, is test-driven. The more time spent in the classroom, it is thought, the better chance of high scores (this is both realistic and true when memorization is the key to success). Many middle and high school students, particularly those at the top, spend nearly as much time after school each day in special institutes called

Korean education shines where memorization and "one right answer" styles of teaching and learning are most appropriate . . .

"hak-gwan" or with private tutors as they do in school. The long winter and summer vacations are opportunities for parents to enroll their children in special classes, lest they fall behind other students. Children entering even second grade of elementary school are given summer homework and projects. One Seoul high school was known a few years ago to assign required "extra classes" for all but nine days of the five-week-long summer vacation! Elementary students usually are assigned extended projects to complete during vacation periods, as well. While this type of thing is looked upon with disdain by parents who want desperately for their children to enjoy some time of rest, they have no real choice but to go along, fearing that to buck the system might put their child at an educational disadvantage. Such single-minded focus on raising individual or schoolwide scores on standardized tests is neither unusual nor surprising. Education is both one of Korea's greatest assets and its greatest societal flaws. We could attribute this to contemporary Korea's race to be competitive in a new, global market, but this national educational frenzy is nothing new. Hendrik Hamel, a Dutch sailor who had the misfortune to be shipwrecked on Cheju Island off the southern coast of Korea in 1653, reported that Koreans indulged in a "national devotion to education." He reported that he observed both aristocrats and those of lesser status "take great care of the Education of their Children, and put them very young to learn to read and write, to which the Nation is much addicted." (Cumings, p. 60) Education has a long and sacred tradition in Korea!

Some idea of the modern version of what Hamel observed can be experienced best during the season of college entrance exams, occurring each November across Korea. (The Korean school year begins in February or early March and runs through the following December.) Below are excerpts from two newspaper articles from November 1997, one written the day before the exams, the other on the day after.

Tomorrow's college
entrance exam educational event of the year

(The Korea Herald, November 18, 1997, by Shin Hye-son, staff reporter)

This time annually, the nation experiences the most important educational event of the year; state-run college entrance exams. Nearly 890,000 mainly high school senior students will take, as it is officially referred to, the College Scholastic Ability Test at 820 test sites nationwide tomorrow.

Exam scores, along with high school grades, are the most important factors that colleges and universities look at in deciding which students to grand admission to.

As in previous years, this important day concerns government agencies, as well as students and parents. Mothers and fathers have been seen praying at temples and churches for their siblings [sic] success.

Government agencies announced a number of steps to ensure that the test will be carried out without glitches. . . Airline takeoffs and landings will be banned nationwide from 8:35 a.m. to 9:00 a.m. and from 4:05 p.m. to 4:35 p.m. to ensure jet roars do not disturb students during the English and Korean listening comprehension portion of the exam tomorrow.

Employees at government agencies and many private companies have been told to report to work at 10 a.m., about one hour later than normal, so students will not get caught in often horrendous rush-hour traffic. . . Extra taxis, subway trains and traffic police will also be mobilized.

The media also carried articles providing practical advice for the test and tidbits such as the best food to eat and the optimum time to wake up.

Stores selling goods aimed at wishing test-takers good luck, such as sticky taffy or " yot" are prevalent.

56

The entrance exam consists mainly of short-answer and multiple choice questions, and is the vortex of the educational system.

Many parents regard a good test performance and subsequent admissions to a top college as a guarantee to future high-caliber employment and prosperity, and a notable position in society.

Students often begin exam preparation as early as their high school freshman year, even attending lessons with private tutors and at educational institutions.

Those who don' t get into the university they want, sometimes take a year off to try again, and prepare for the following year' s test.

Test results are to be announced Dec. 20.

Two days later, the following article appeared:

College entrance exam held nationwide

(The Korea Herald, November 20, 1997)

Hundreds of thousands of high school seniors are greatly relieved now that the state-run college exam is over. . . .

To help the day go smoothly, police and military officials deployed extra patrol cars and motorcycles near major subway stations, and even transported late-comers to test sites. Exam participants were greeted at the gates of sites by younger high school students, who had arrived there early in the morning despite the cold weather, waiting for their seniors. . . . The sense of relief was also shared by professors, teachers and other support personnel mobilized to prepare questions for the college entrance exam.

Headed by Prof. So Kwang-sop of Seoul National University, the 183-member team was released yesterday afternoon from their 30-day-long confinement in a hotel in Yongin, Kyonggi Province.

Since Oct. 20, they had been there in complete isolation, not allowed contact with the outside world to prevent leakage of test information. They wrestled with 5,000 books, sources for questions.

During that period, security was tight at the hotel. All elevators and stairways leading to the floors of the rooms, where 72 professors and 47 high school teachers stayed, were sealed, and armed policemen conducted watertight patrols around the hotel.

No exception was made, even for Education Minister Lee Myung-hyun, who visited the hotel to encourage the professors and teachers Nov. 9. He was thoroughly checked by police.

The National Board for Educational Evaluation in charge of supervising the college entrance exam said that the one-month procedure cost 500 million won ($500,000).

Test results will be announced Dec. 20. (SHS)

Why is there such an emphasis on education and college entrance scores that airlines, the military, and police become involved? Why is there such pressure to know what will be on the test that test-writers must be sealed off from society for a month lest they leak questions? Why does Korea still experience the "addiction" reported by Hamel 350 years ago?

The answer is simple. Today, as in the past, one who is educated has the doors opened to the higher echelons of society; an uneducated person is relegated to the very bottom of society. The only difference is that today the opportunity for education is open to all rather than just to the male aristocracy. Ironically, one reason for this emphasis on higher education is that the South Korean population is over-educated. Without a college education, one can hardly get a clerk's job in a corporation or bank. There is intense competition for such spots, however. Only recently has entrepreneurship become possible and popular, particularly in the high tech area; joining a conglomerate is still the preferred route for many.

Not only is having a college diploma critically important, but also *where* that diploma comes from is critical to future success. As is true in the social structure of Korea, there is a strict hierarchy in the educational system. Ask any Mr. Kim in the street which Korean university is the "best," and he will undoubtedly answer "Seoul National University." When considering which university would be best for a student, there is little discussion as to his or her abilities, talents, or interests. Nor is there any discussion about the strengths or weakness of a particular department at a particular university unless one is highly talented in a specialized academic area such as art or music. Name brand is all-important to the applicant and to his or her worried family; simply and finally, Seoul National is the "best." Interesting and understandable is the frequent answer given when a Korean is asked what U. S. university is the "best." Without hesitation, he or she will almost certainly answer "Harvard." Other famous supposed Ivy League colleges are also acceptable, including Stanford and M.I.T.! Unfortunately, schools such as Dartmouth and Brown are not well known, and are often not known to be "Ivy League," and are therefore not as high in the Korean hierarchy. There is no question but that any non-Ivy League school would be considered to be of "inferior" quality. Just below Seoul National in this strict hierarchy are Yonsei and Koryo Universities (and the all-women's Ewha University), with a few other Seoul universities following in third.

Finally, there are the universities that are nearly everyone's third, fourth, or last choices. Until very recently, it was impossible to apply to more than one university in a particular level in a given year. Thus, choosing which college to attend was an all-or-nothing exercise. Many students, failing

SEOUL NATIONAL UNIVERSITY

KOREA AND YONSEI UNIVERSITIES

ANY UNIVERSITIES IN SEOUL

"THE REST"

KOREA'S "HIGHER EDUCATION PYRAMID"

entrance to the college of their choice, become full-time students for a year, cramming for the next year's exam in hopes that they can earn a coveted seat.

Why is entrance to a *particular* university so important? First, because once in a school, one does not transfer between universities. Just as people do not change companies during their career, students do not transfer, they remain part of their "group." Transferring is just not part of the Korean educational system. Secondly, the name of the school on a diploma is very important to future life. Certain large corporations hire most entirely from a particular university, normally the university from which the founder of the corporation was graduated. Earlier we mentioned the life-long importance of peer relationships made in high school and college. Certainly, it would be more advantageous to build contacts and close interdependent relationships with those who are headed for positions of power and influence (from their elite university) than with people whose backgrounds were from lower down on the educational hierarchy. The selection of a university can carry directly over into future personal, as well as professional, life. When it comes time to choose a spouse (often a good number of years after college, after military service for males, and after getting settled in life), importance is placed on where one went to school. A graduate of Seoul National, Yonsei, or Ewha Universities would be marrying far "below" themselves if their intended was from a provincial or lower-level school.

Simply put, *which* college one attends can and does have lifelong effects on future employment possibilities, social group, prestige, and even future marriage partner. To a much greater degree than is normal except in very elite universities in the West, in Korea education represents more than learning. It is without doubt a highly prized social pedigree.

It is interesting to note that although there is tremendous pressure to study hard to get *into* an all-important name university, once a student enters, regardless of the prestige or name of the university, it is nearly impossible to "flunk out." Professors are hesitant to fail students, even those who seldom show up for class. Little emphasis is placed on academics and a great deal on social life, that is, on establishing relationships. There are signs that this is slowly changing as there is more and more competition for employment after graduation, and employers are looking more and more closely at how well a student did at university (*what* he or she knows) rather than *who* he or she has gotten to know. Most college professors, though, could readily tell stories of pressure brought on them by those above in the hierarchy not to fail students who did virtually nothing to earn a passing grade.

Until the Korean educational system changes in very some basic ways, there is no other way for a student to succeed but to do everything possible to get ahead of his or her peers. This will most likely not happen until classes shrink to a size that allows discussion and the interplay of ideas, until Confucianism and the rigid respect for the way things have always been done is set aside, and until enough Korean children and educators are able to experience Western education that parents won't tolerate this rigid system any longer. This is already being seen by the tremendous pressure for and interest in enrolling children in foreign (mostly American) boarding schools, even at the elementary level. Perhaps Korean education will earn the reputation it already undeservingly enjoys in many Western countries when its existing characteristics of hard work, a structured curriculum, and a respect for teachers is energized by a synergy with creativity, individualistic thinking, and encouragement of diversity. At that point Korea may well have an unbeatable blend of the best of Eastern and Western education.

How does all this affect the Korean student in an international school? For students who are planning to attend university outside of Korea, the influence is indirect. Their parents are carrying with them their memory of what a "good" student is, of what it takes to get into a "good" university, and what kind of name brand university is acceptable. They may not understand how non-Korean higher education is different, and not realize that they are actually fostering habits and ways of thought that may be working against their children's present and future academic success. (More on that later.)

Secondly, for students who will be returning to Korea for university, it is a reality. They truly do have to study and memorize. They do have to cram for Korean exams while also taking a full load of studies at an international school. They know that they will be "behind" their compatriots when they return home, even if they now have the very important skills of English fluency and the ability to "think outside the box." It is important for the international educator to understand that excelling and doing everything possible to come out on top is truly of crucial importance for these students. They are being handicapped by being in our schools rather than in Korean schools where their future peers are working overtime to earn coveted spots in a top university. The fact that often the methods they may use to get to the top conflict head-on with many international schools' educational philosophies and goals is of little concern to the student and parent. They know that their future lies in Korea, and that they will not be ready for that future if they fully adapt to a Western educational philosophy.

Finally, international educators must realize that parents will make tremendous sacrifices — financial, social, or otherwise — to get their child into the university of choice either in Korea or overseas. They recognize that their children's attendance at an international school gives them a chance of getting into a Western university and avoiding Korean higher education, a chance they possibly never got. Given the chance that their child might be able to go to Harvard or Yale or M.I.T., then, they will do everything in their power to be sure that that happens. Yes, the child might have to suffer long hours of study. Yes, the parents might go into debt. Yes, the child may be interested in something totally different than that which the parents see in the future, but if the chance is there, they will go for it. Unfortunately, many go about it in ways totally appropriate in Korea, but that sometimes result in failure or even tragedy in a Western educational setting. As educators who are working with the children of ethnic Koreans, this becomes a challenge for us. In trying to instill such Western educational values as being well-rounded and being able to think critically, creatively, and independently we are confronting an educational culture five thousand years old. We can become frustrated, for despite our best intentions and sincere attempts, the tendency of many Korean parents is to conform to Korean educational norms and values, and to question the advice of people other than Koreans in an area of life as critical as education.

We should also understand that when we deal with an ethnic Korean family we are not dealing with only parents and a child, but often with the expectations and dreams of grandparents, the demands of the extended family, and the consensus of the Korean community, particularly the mothers

64

of that community. Quite often critical decisions regarding the Western education of their children are made from very considered, very sincere, very serious, but very misinformed positions. Often, these would be very appropriate decisions were they made in the Korean educational context. In the Western context, however, they are often very detrimental to a child and to his or her education. It is the responsibility of international educators to do their best to educate parents in these areas. This is not easy; in trusting us, a parent is putting aside what he or she knows to be true in Korea, and gambling the future of a son or daughter on the words and opinions of a foreigner — an outsider.

Most ethnic Korean adults we find in the admissions offices of our international schools today share the historical, cultural, and educational backgrounds discussed up to now. However, life experiences after leaving Korea also shape the perceptions, values, and ideals of these individuals. There are three major experiences by which ethnic Koreans may find themselves molded: an immigrant experience, an international experience, and a returnee experience. It is to these experiences that we now turn our attention.

TIME TO THINK. . .

What educational characteristics mentioned here do you see in your students? Have any of your questions been answered? Have new questions been raised?

What can you learn from your students about what motivates them educationally?

What characteristics mentioned here don't fit some of your students? Why might this be?

What do you know about the educational plans of your students? Are any headed back to Korea? If they are headed to North America or Europe, what are their plans? Can you or your guidance department help them to make logical choices? How much are they making decisions based on reality, and how much on parental dreams?

How do the educational characteristics of your ethnic Korean students affect the academic climate of your school? What opportunities do they present to the school? What challenges do they bring? How might you address them?

THE SACRIFICE OF A KOREAN MOTHER

The author has known her for over twenty-five years. At age 81, Kim Soon-im is a stately and confident, yet tired Korean grandmother. She gave birth to three sons and two daughters, and raised them well while being a caring and dutiful wife. What amazes me, though, is the dedication that she showed over the years in pursuit of education for her and her husband' s extended families. While she had a full house of her own, she also throughout her marriage was mother to 26 other relatives' children for months or even years at a time. Although her husband was well-employed as an engineer, sometimes there were not enough rice bowls to go around, and the children had to eat in shifts. Why was her house so full?

Kim Soon-im and her husband had left the deep south Korean countryside to move to the port city of Masan shortly after the Korean War. There her children had access to city education, which in those days was much higher in quality than "country" education. Country relatives sent their children to live with the family to share in that opportunity. There was little in the way of payment other than an occasional bag of rice from the farm; after all, everybody was "f amily." It never occurred to her to say that the house was full enough. Relatives would do the same for her children were the shoe on the other foot. She had what her relatives lacked: keys to a city education and a brighter future for her children. She had a family obligation to share those keys. She fulfilled it with dignity, and it is her proud legacy.

CHAPTER V: INDIVIDUAL EXPERIENCES

Immigrants, Sojourners, Returnees, and TCK's

Up to this point, we have discussed the historical, cultural, and educational backgrounds common to the majority of our ethnic Korean parents and their children. Now, however, we will look at influences that affect only certain of our students. The only way to know what experiences apply to whom is to ask the students themselves. Are they Korean citizens, "straight from Korea," but living overseas with the intention of returning? Are they first or second-generation immigrants? If you are in teaching Korea, which of your students are somewhat Westernized "returnees," which are truly foreign children of parent returnees, and which are fully Korean children who are simply attending an international school? How have these different experiences molded these children?

The Immigrant Experience

As noted earlier, many ethnic Korean children living outside Korea and most Korean-American (Korean-Canadian, Korean-German, etc.) students living in Korea are the children of immigrants. The parents' and children's views of their own identities have been molded by their immigrant experiences, whatever their adopted country. No longer do they see themselves as purely "Korean," although they may identify themselves as such. The longer they have lived outside of Korea the more they have become acculturated to their new

68

country and to the Western culture, particularly after beginning school.

Whether living outside of Korea or having returned with their foreign children, these people — our students' parents — have had or are having the experience of being new immigrants. For most immigrants from Korea, their adopted nations have lured them as "lands of promise" rather than "lands of opportunity." They suffered the long waits and not infrequent indignities of the immigration process, from standing in long "visa lines" in Seoul to a possibly less than friendly welcome in their new neighborhood. For example, those who have gone to the United States might have had a Hollywood image of the U.S. before departure, which of course may clash with the reality of long work days and difficult living situations in their new home. They may have expected instant riches, as well as gunfights on every corner, but have found neither. Job discrimination, usually based on cultural differences or lack of English ability, but sometimes blatantly racial, may have kept them from advancing through business ranks unless they limited their sights to strictly Korean-run businesses. It is not unusual to find a graduate from a "top" Korean university operating a grocery or liquor store to support the family, with all of the family working 18-hour days, struggling to ensure that the children receive a "top" American education. Although initially after immigrating they might have felt that they were advancing quickly through the economic ranks, eventually they may have reached a point of economic frustration, a glass ceiling beyond which they could not go. This often occurs about fifteen years after arrival, and can lead to frustration and depression at the lack of unlimited opportunity in their new country. The individual may become convinced that the "promise" of the adopted land was a sham. Most, however, decide to stick it out and dream of their children fulfilling their own now tarnished aspirations. They want to live their dreams of the West vicariously through their children.

Many Korean immigrants to North America in the Seventies and early Eighties became quite acculturated to their adopted society. There were few Korean communities, and learning English and local cultural norms was imperative. In more recent years in the United States, however, as the number of ethnic Koreans has risen (over 800,000 at present) it is becoming less and less necessary for Korean-Americans, especially in some of the larger Korean communities such as in Los Angeles, New York, or Chicago, to become acculturated. They may tend to "ghetto" themselves, living totally "Korean-style," neglecting to learn English, even holding on to those Korean values and expectations which might be hindrances to success in America. Their children follow generations of immigrant children who suffer both generational and cultural gaps with their parents. Relationships with parents may become problematic: as the children grow up proficient in English, they sometimes lose respect for their parents as parents come to depend on them for help in English to survive. An interesting subgroup among immigrant teens and young adults is what is called the "il-chum-oh," or "1.5" generation. They are neither first nor second-generation ethnic Koreans, having immigrated as teenagers. They have a core of Korean values and language learned in childhood covered by a veneer of Western characteristics. They do not fit in comfortably with either their Korean parents or other new immigrants, who seem old fashioned or "too Korean." On the other hand, they do not fit in with their much more Westernized younger brothers and sisters or peers. Often their English is imperfect, yet they can't speak, read, or write age-appropriate Korean, either. They may find solace only in others like themselves, and find themselves in conflict with both first and second-generation immigrant Koreans.

Many Korean immigrants truly want for their children to become active participants in the culture of their new country wherever it may be. Others, however, want them to remain Korean in all but citizenship. They want their children to keep Korean culture and values alive, to speak Korean fluently, and to marry Korean spouses, all the while profiting from greater economic and educational opportunities than they might find in Korea. While the desire for many Koreans to expect their child to attend only an "Ivy League" university (a term that is used with great ease and greater misunderstanding among Koreans, as we saw earlier) is well documented, in fairness we must state that this phenomenon is not limited to Koreans. Many Vietnamese and Indians also share this characteristic, and previous groups of immigrants whose cultures have held education in high regard (earlier Jewish immigrants, for example) also held such high expectations. It is interesting to note that such very high educational expectations for any immigrant group have generally lasted about one generation; it remains to be seen whether ethnic Koreans will follow the same path.

For those readers who are teaching immigrant children or foreign-born children of immigrants, how much of what you have just read will apply depends on a variety of factors: the age of the parents at immigration, the age of the children at immigration, whether or not the family plans to return to Korea, whether the family lives in a Korean community or has more fully acculturated, parents' educational level, and many other factors. Getting to know the children and their parents, their history, and their backgrounds is crucial to understanding the children as students.

71

THE INTERNATIONAL OVERSEAS EXPERIENCE:
Korean Children as Sojourners

Since the mid-1980's Korea has become an increasingly important and involved member of the international community. Korean conglomerates have plants and offices all over the world, staffed by Korean executives and engineers who bring their families with them. Korean Christian churches are sending out missionaries by the thousands, as well. By April 2003 there were as many as 10,000 Korean adult missionaries with as many as 5000 school-aged children, serving primarily in the central Asian nations formerly part of the Soviet Union, in China, and in the Philippines. In addition, thousands of Korean students and educators are studying and teaching around the globe. The children of many of these "Korean expatriates" are found in international schools. In some locales there may be only one or two ethnic Korean families. In cities or remote work sites where an organization has a substantial presence, however, Koreans may make up a large proportion of the student population. In just the past five or six years, one American-style international school in China has gone from only a few percent to fully half of its students coming directly from Korea. Numbers like this from any one national group are bound to seriously impact any school's program and culture.

Many of these children that we find in international schools become what are known as "Third Culture Kids," or "TCK's." TCK's are defined as being either 1) mobile children who are growing up in cultures different from either their nation of citizenship or that of the culture of their parents, or 2) those who are growing up in an international school and social culture even though they may live in their parents' home culture. For example, an Korean child living in Uzbekistan with his missionary or corporate parents is a TCK. An American or German child growing up in Korea would similarly be a TCK. An ethnic Korean child attending an international school in Korea would also be a TCK by virtue of the fact that he or she is experiencing a mobile, international culture. (For an excellent, in-depth study of the characteristics of TCK's both as children and later as adults, see *The Third Culture Kid Experience: Growing Up Among Worlds*, by David C. Pollock and Ruth E. Van Reken. These authors describe a number of characteristics shared by most TCK's, whatever their national background). We will see in Chapter VI that, as is true for most TCK's, an overseas experience for a Korean child can be a double-edged sword. For example, by attending an international school, the child avoids, at least for part of his or her education, the grueling Korean system. While this is a real plus in many ways (one which many Korean students and parents would give anything for) it is also a real negative if and when the child returns to Korea and enters Korean school. The very rigidity of the Korean system and the difficulty the system and culture have in accepting diversity work against the re-entry adjustment of returning students. In addition, the more the child or family has acculturated to the foreign or international culture, the less fit they are to return to the strict Korean society, with its emphasis on harmony and conformity. Conversely, the more able they will be as adults to succeed in the larger international community. They may lose their sense of being Korean and find themselves in an increasingly wide cultural gap with their parents. Their parents may fear that their children are becoming too "foreign."

> *. . . an overseas experience for a Korean child can be a double-edged sword.*

While learning English in an international school, these children will not fit in totally with the new school environment and may feel left out. If there are enough Korean children in the school they may seek out soul mates, those who understand what they are going through, and who know what together they will face when they return to Korea. A common theme heard from teachers of overseas Korean students is that they seem exclusive and cliquish. This often occurs if there are enough Korean students to maintain a viable group. A strong sense of nationalism, a common language, a tendency to be a member of a cohesive group, and the exclusion faced by many ESL students anywhere support this. They may also think that teachers don't understand them — and they may be right. Hopefully books like this will help somewhat in those situations.

THE "RETURNEE" EXPERIENCE:
"Coming Home" or a "Hidden Immigrant"?

Many overseas ethnic Korean families return to Korea to live either temporarily or permanently. What are the reasons for this "return migration?" There are as many answers to that question as there are families. Some who went to the West to study for a few years as undergraduates or graduate students just stayed on, married other Koreans, and settled down in their new countries, becoming "educational immigrants." Others who intentionally emigrated to the West may have tired of the immigrant experience. Their dream of success in their adopted country may have gone sour, or a sense of duty to aging parents may have demanded their return to Korea. As they enter their mid-thirties, their parents would be approaching sixty, the age at which Koreans are considered honorable elders, and at which their children are expected to begin taking care of them. Others may return due to the lure of new job opportunities in Korea, free of the social burden of being "immigrants." Others might be homesick. Of course, for many overseas non-immigrant Koreans the reason for going overseas was job related and their term of a few years of overseas service has simply ended.

Whatever their reason for returning to Korea, both parents and children share certain common experiences. For example, children are often considered by parents and extended family members to be "returning" to Korea, but in fact they may have never lived there. They are, unlike their parents, moving to a foreign, although possibly somewhat familiar, country. Ironically, parents of Korean children overseas who have worked very hard to be sure to carry on Korean culture and traditions in their family may find that, due to the rapidly changing culture of Korea, they are more traditional and "Korean" than their relatives and friends "back home" where things have changed dramatically in the past twenty years.

The ethnic Korean child faces a difficult situation should his or her family, for whatever reason, return to Korea. He or she has been exposed to the pluralism of Western culture, lifestyles and standards, and has acquired fluency in English. He or she has truly become a hyphenated Korean, a mix of rich Korean cultural and linguistic characteristics and valuable Western characteristics and attitudes. Many of the qualities that meant "success" in the non-Korean culture or international school environment were fostered and cultivated by parents and the school. Some of these characteristics become negatives, however, when the plane touches down at Incheon Airport. The firm handshake or look in the eye may offend grandfather. Grandmother may consider a girl's wide

smile and ready laugh or dark makeup to be unladylike –
"nice girls" don't do those things. The child's practiced bow
of greeting may not be quite deep enough for the grandparents; his spoken Korean possibly childish (which makes it
rude due to the levels of Korean language) and unacceptable;
her hairstyle or clothes too extreme. They may not have
learned the more polite formal body language a native-born
Korean child would have learned naturally. An outgoing,
gregarious, confident, fun-loving and inquisitive nature may
not be appreciated in a nation where children are to be first
and foremost successful and serious students. Suddenly this
well-adjusted young person quite often finds him or herself
the object of loving but open ridicule by relatives and other
Koreans, and quickly realizes that being American or Canadian or German or having lived overseas is not appreciated or
valued in Korea, and in fact may be the root of social unac-
ceptability. He or she is not considered to be a "foreigner" by
relatives, but rather a poorly mannered and ill-adjusted Korean. Parents often become the object of blame — "Why did
you bring me here?" is a common theme. The children become what Pollock and Van Reken call "hidden immigrants."
They look like they belong, they are treated as if they belong,
but they do not belong — this in a nation in which belonging
is of tremendous importance! Complicating this may be parental realization that their child is no longer truly Korean,
and parents may do everything possible to re-acculturate
them by enrolling them in special institutes or by hiring tutors. Many are put in Korean schools and are just expected to
"sink or swim."

Not only are the *children* facing culture shock and possible ridicule, but parents as well are suddenly expected to act
totally Korean and possibly take on the role of obedient children to aged parents. For fathers, life may become more

pleasant, with new opportunities for professional and social advancement opening up. However, the Korean business culture demands long hours, including working until seven or eight o'clock at night (or until the boss leaves) and a half day on Saturdays, with business "golf" meetings on Sundays. After work, there are often obligatory dinners out with fellow workers or visiting customers, not ending until everyone has had far too much to drink. More then one "returnee" marriage has reached a crisis when dad starts to come home drunk in the wee hours. The Western family tradition of "dad home by five, dinner at six, and some family time afterwards" too often quickly disappears, with dad seldom (and unpredictably) returning home before very late in the evening. Only recently has there been a growing realization in the Korean business culture that husbands have responsibilities to the family in addition to bringing home a fat paycheck, but this is only slowly developing. Too often a couple who has developed and grown in a Western-style marriage finds that due to the husband's job demands, their marriage is taking on a less intimate, sharing atmosphere. Children see less and less of their fathers, and mothers take on a much more central and "Korean mother's" role with the children.

The children become what Pollock and Van Reken call "hidden immigrants." They look like they belong, they are treated as if they belong, but they do not belong.

The situation for mothers may be more difficult. If a woman never became acculturated to the West, it may be easy, even a relief, to come "home" to Korea. If she became somewhat Westernized, however, she is now in a cultural dilemma, realizing that she no longer really "fits" in Korea.

Many are the Korean moms who have admitted, "I always felt like an outsider in America, because I knew I was different. Now I feel like an outsider in Korea, because everyone else tells me I'm different. I'm not sure that I belong anywhere." A young Canadian-Korean teacher states, "It's ironic. I find that I feel Canadian when I'm in Korea and more Korean when I'm in Canada."

Old college friends tell the returning Korean mom that somehow she is different, that she speaks and dresses and holds herself like a foreigner. Other mothers' intense discussion of their own children's education and upcoming exams and expensive tutors makes her realize that she has little in common with them, and she may begin to feel guilty that by taking her children overseas she has put them behind the children of her old friends, and has robbed them of the pride of being Korean.

> *"I always felt like an outsider in America, because I knew I was different. Now I feel like an outsider in Korea, because everyone else tells me I'm different. I'm not sure that I belong anywhere."*

A further dynamic for "returning" mothers is that often they must resume the role of daughter-in-law that they have not practiced since they left Korea, possibly as young brides. Due to the tremendously inflated real estate prices in Korea, many returning families who lived well overseas may be forced to live with in-laws for a while. Given the very strong bonds between a Korean son and his mother, even in adulthood, a whole new set of family dynamics may emerge, particularly if the mother-in-law does not understand the cultural changes that her son and his wife have experienced while living outside Korea. This may bode ill for the daughter-in-law, particularly if she becomes the object of blame for not bringing up her "Korean" children "properly," adding to her feelings of alienation and incompetence.

A result of these radical changes in lifestyle is that the somewhat Westernized mothers often turn to others who will understand their predicament — other ethnic Korean mothers suffering the same adjustments. As mentioned earlier, teachers and administrators in international schools in Korea may realize that informal grade level "Korean mothers' clubs" develop as support groups — both to help members deal with their alienation to Korea and to provide information and support in matters related to the "foreign" school system into which they have placed their children. (Similar groups or clubs may form among overseas Koreans whose children attend international schools). If these moms are knowledgeable about the school's culture, aims, and values, positive communication can result, with those less acculturated to Western education benefiting from those who are more so. However, peer pressure and an age-based (or husbands' position-based) hierarchy that develops within the groups may result in solidarity of opinion based on misinformation or misunderstanding that may not be healthy for either the school or the children. A teacher or administrator, in trying to deal with a difficult academic or behavioral situation, may find that he or she is not just dealing with the child's parents, but with the solidarity and opinion of the mother's social group to which she may have gone for advice. These groups may become vehicles for comparisons of report card grades, honor role status, and SAT results, even of the children of moms not in the group. Gossip regarding teachers and other families can rage, not so much about personal family issues (as might be true in the West) but about whose child is at the top of the class, who got in trouble at school (and thus who to keep one's own child away from), who got accepted at what college (and who didn't), what teacher is the "best" in the seventh grade, etc., etc. This unhealthy situation can and does result in a great deal of competition among mothers based on children's grades, summer school plans, and college acceptances. The need to conform to the opinion of the group in order to be accepted may be overwhelming for some mothers.

It is important to remember that each returning family's priorities and dreams are different. One family might wish to remain as Westernized and international as possible while being in Korea and plan on the children going to university in the West and eventually settling there. They want their children to attend an international school where they can continue to enjoy the benefits of a Western education and learn to be truly bicultural. Others want their children to learn to become Korean, but realizing the demands and limited opportunities of the Korean educational system, and recognizing that their children could never survive

It is important to remember that each returning family's priorities and dreams are different.

entering at the middle or high school level, they wish to enroll their children in international schools in Korea. For this group, many of their core values and plans for their children's future may be at odds with those of international, Western-style schools. They may be in disagreement as to standards of discipline, study habits, teaching styles, or expectations of individual freedom and responsibility. With such basic differences, why would they send them to international schools? Unfortunately, they may simply want the faster and easier route to Western higher education and its status than Korean education provides.

Other families may want their children to go to Korean school to "learn to be Korean" while maintaining their Western language and cultural background. If such a family maintains contacts in the West, visiting during school vacations, going to camp or summer school, watching English language television, and reading age-appropriate books, these children can become truly bicultural.

Still other families may have never planned on staying out of Korea as long as they did, and consider themselves and their children to be completely Korean. They have no intention of their children remaining Westernized. Often these children, after an initial adjustment period, succeed quite well in Korean school and quickly take on a Korean identity. Others, particularly if they have become totally Westernized, suffer difficulty in academics as well as harassment by other children and even teachers who do not understand that they are going through a major adjustment in culture, and view them simply as uncultured and rude Koreans. Often these children suffer terribly. The quotes on page 92 by students who have made the switch to Korean schools are somewhat dated, being from the mid-1980's, but while some of the specifics might be different today, the basic issues remain the same.

Most truly Korean families returning to Korea today do not have the choice of choosing a Western-style education, however. Children who are Korean citizens may find themselves required by law to attend Korean schools. Although the Korean government has recently taken some steps that open up the option of international education for a few "international" Korean children who have spent an extended time outside Korea, most must attend Korean schools. Whether or not the family wants or is legally eligible to send their children to a Western-style school in Korea, though, enrollment pressure has required some international schools in

Korea to limit new admissions to those who are truly non-Korean in both citizenship and culture, thus making ineligible for admission many children of Korean citizenship who have lived overseas. Given the choice of no school or Korean school, it is often better for these children if they are of middle or high school age to go to boarding schools outside Korea to finish an English language education.

It can be seen, then, that upon arrival in Korea, a crucial decision may have to be made for the children that will have lifelong ramifications — that of whether or not a child should enter a Korean school or attend a Western-style international school. A primary school student, even if his or her Korean is poor, can most likely make the transition to Korean school and see success within two or three years. However, an older child may have a great deal of adjustment to make, both academically and socially, to the Korean school culture. Korean school creates Korean adults; international education creates either Western adults or bicultural adults who eventually are at ease in both the East and the West. Which route to take is a critical family decision affecting not only the child but also the family and the family's future. It is a question of whether or not future generations will be Korean.

Regardless of where they go to school, however, many ethnic Korean young people find themselves caught in difficult educational and cultural dilemmas upon coming to Korea. Their parents are themselves working hard to become "Korean" again, and they are pulling their children along with them. Korean society, from grandmothers to taxi drivers, demands that these young people act and speak Korean in the best Confucian tradition. The longer they live in Korea, the more outwardly acculturated to Korea they probably appear. However, they may feel alone and alienated from their families. Identity issues that emerge at middle and high school age for all children are confounded by additional ethnic or cultural questions. As they constantly try to balance conflicting Korean and Western values, they may temporarily totally reject their Korean identity, or conversely become "super Koreans," rejecting their Western identity. Other ethnic Korean young people like them, caught in the same dilemma, become their soul mates. Close and lasting friendships develop based on a shared, often painful, experience. Much as their mothers seek out others with similar backgrounds and challenges, understandable survival strategies appear among their children. Unfortunately, to Western educators many of these characteristics appear to be cliquishness, exclusivity, or alienation from non-ethnic Korean students.

The economic collapse of the Asian Rim in 1997 brought new and difficult dilemmas to the parents of overseas Korean children. First, the nation suffered terrific blows to its pride. The oft-touted Korean economic dragon was exposed as empty, supported only by a web of entangled corporate debts and political cover-up and intrigue. Some Korean employees overseas suddenly found themselves without jobs — or even a ticket home, if the company they worked for yesterday disappeared last night. Unemployment raged at record levels in Korea. In 1998 nearly 10,000 people a day were losing their jobs — hardly good news to an out-of-work executive. The catastrophic drop in exchange rates meant that if overseas pay was denominated in Korean currency, the equivalent in terms of foreign currency on which a family must live overseas might have dropped more than 100% in a period of two weeks in late 1997. Mergers and acquisitions meant fewer mid-level corporate jobs, and troubled companies often had to make quick decisions to cease overseas operations and bring employees and their families back home. Many of these families had children attending international schools around the world. Although the Korean economy has nearly recovered (2003), it still has some bumps ahead, and there has been tremendous restructuring, especially in overseas operations. The future remains uncertain; some of the very largest conglomerates with worldwide operations, such as Kia and Daewoo, have tottered and fallen.

KOREAN CHILDREN AS THIRD CULTURE KIDS

Before we finish discussing the returnee experience for overseas children, let's take a look at how the overseas experience affects ethnic Korean children as Third Culture Kids, or TCK's. The characteristics below are discussed in detail by Pollock and Van Reken (see list of resources).

1. Most TCK's have an opportunity to learn a number of languages, including English. This is a real plus for children returning to Korea to study. Foreign language institutes are found in almost every neighborhood in Korea, and children as young as three and four are enrolled in English language programs. Korea is a nation trying hard to communicate with the rest of the world. Returning to Korea fluent in English can give students a real edge in school, although they may be held suspect by their foreign language teachers whose language ability is often far below that of their returning students. This can cause some uneasiness and even jealousy for teachers who are accustomed to being the unchallenged font of all answers. Overall, however, high English scores on the all-important college entrance test give students a strong advantage, and may help to balance weaknesses in other academic areas.

2. Most TCK's develop cross cultural skills, high cultural flexibility, a three-dimensional worldview, and an international orientation. Korea is succeeding in becoming an involved and respected member of the international community. For this to continue the nation needs individuals who can operate from a wider perspective than that of someone who has always lived in a small, monocultural nation. While returned TCK's eventually become vanguards in the national race for internationalism, the TCK experience may in the short term be responsible for these young people's not fitting in well in a nation rife with nationalism and xenophobia. Having cross-cultural skills and an international perspective often means being able to see a situation from both sides. However, being able to express other than purely national or Korean perspectives on issues may land the young person in hot water with new friends who may see him or her as being disloyal to Korea or Korea's position in world affairs. They are not unique among TCK's in this regard, who often experience this problem when they return to a "home" where they may have never lived and where they feel like outsiders.

3. TCK's tend to be mature for their age due to their experiences. This is a real plus if the student returns to college in Korea. Korean college students have had one goal in life up until that time, and that has been to be a student. Life skills, independence, personal initiative, and common sense are often lacking. They all too often simply look to their "seniors" for clues to how to behave. Many TCK's of whatever nationality are more able to resist temptation, make informed judgments, and behave in mature ways than their peers who have never lived outside their home country. On the other hand, if they have not lived in Korea during their teenage years, they may be naive to the youth culture and in

85

ways to stay out of trouble. Just as a Canadian TCK might feel "out of it" and uncertain when moving to Canada, so might a Korean TCK upon "returning" to Korea. He or she must quickly learn to "be Korean" in order to fit in and not be the nail that sticks up.

4. *TCK families tend to be close, especially if they have moved from country to country.* Korean families are already close, with strong parental/child ties, a tradition of caring and respect, and a sense of history tied to ancestors. The general TCK characteristic of family closeness may be magnified in a Korean family, although this could possibly be negatively balanced by the growing cultural differences between parents and children.

SPECIAL NOTES REGARDING RETURNING KOREAN CITIZEN STUDENTS

As noted earlier, most students of Korean citizenship are required to return to Korean schools upon their return to Korea. Until a few years ago, there were so few returning children that they were quietly absorbed into the Korean educational system with little or no consideration for their background, special talents, or difficulties. However, in the last few years the Korean Ministry of Education has recognized that such children are quite different than most Korean children. The general attitude has been to re-acculturate them as quickly as possible, although there are very few special programs for them. Most enroll in Korean schools and do the best they can. There have been some attempts to create some "Korean international schools" within the public school system, but these to date have been Korean schools in every way except that a few courses are taught in English or other languages. Often TCK high school students enroll in special high schools that specialize in teaching foreign languages, where they can focus on this strength. At this point (spring, 2003) a child who has attended international schools for five or more years outside of Korea is legally eligible to attend international schools in Korea, but due to the high demand by true expatriates for spaces in international schools, particularly in Seoul, this is not always an option. As more and more Korean children return to Korea after extended sojourns overseas, it will be interesting to see how Korea, only now beginning to value their overseas experiences, responds. Certainly it must, and changes in laws and regulations will occur. The best advice international educators can give Korean parents when they have questions as to their child's educational options in Korea is to have them contact the education office in the city to which they will return, or individual international schools if they are looking at that option.

The situation for students entering college is somewhat more positive, although still cloudy. Some colleges give extra points on entrance exams to students who are native speakers of other languages or give extra admission "points" to certain returnees and foreigners, recognizing that those students will bring a more international view to their student body. The entire situation surrounding both the legality of Korean citizen children attending non-Korean schools and the status of admission of TCK Koreans to various Korean universities is currently (Spring 2003) evolving and very fluid. Parents should contact the Ministry of Education (not individual embassies) to get up-to-date information, as well as the admissions offices of colleges that they wish for their children to attend rather than depend on word of mouth.

CHAPTER VI: SMASHING STEREOTYPES

Looking at Individuals

Up to this point, ethnic Korean children have been described as being the products of their parents' historical, cultural, and educational backgrounds. We have also taken a look at the experiences of international life as well as those of returning to Korea or moving to Korea for the first time. A stereotypical picture has been painted of Korean children who are being molded by many of the same forces and turning out all the same. This is hardly the whole story, however. While it is true that the *backgrounds* of many such children have some striking similarities due to the homogeneity of the Korean culture, it is just as true that the *foreground* of each child's life is painted by his or her individual experience. To what extent any set of parents or any child reflects the characteristics discussed up to now is a result of any number of factors. In working with these young people we need to keep this in mind at all times, lest we paint them all with the same brush. Each child is an individual and deserves to be treated as such. Some children act and think like they never left Cleveland; some act like international TCK's; others may seem like they never left Seoul. As educators we need to ask ourselves some questions about each and every ethnic Korean child who comes into our classrooms if we are truly interested in discovering "Where are they coming from?":

1. Is this the "first time out" for the family? Are they "real" Koreans who are only a flight away from being "at home" in Korea? If so, much of what is included in this book will apply.

2. How long has the child been out of Korean schools?
Was he or she in a classroom in Pusan last week? Have they
always attended school outside of Korea? Don't expect them
to be too "Korean" if their only contact with a Korean school
was to drive by one during summer vacation.

3. How many Korean students do you have in your
school? How strong is the Korean community in your city?
If the children live in an ethnic Korean neighborhood, if they
attend Korean church, or if they attend Saturday and evening
Korean school, then they will maintain their Korean characteristics much more easily than if theirs is one of only a few
Korean families in a larger international community.

4. Are the children hyphenated Koreans (Korean-
American, Korean-Brazilian, Korean-Canadians, etc.)? This
is not a question about a culturally mixed family, but of a
family that emigrated to a foreign country, and whose children are citizens and members of the culture of that nation. If
so, the longer the parents lived there, particularly if they emigrated before they entered their teens, the less Korean they
will be. Sometimes the parents grew up as Third Culture Kids
who may find themselves foreigners in Korea!

5. What is the educational level of the parents, and
where were they educated? Most parents of the children we
find in our schools, be they immigrants or overseas employees of Korean companies, are well educated. Often, one or the
other of the parents speaks English very well. They may have
a strong understanding of Western education due to their
own experience, although usually only at the university level.
They may retain much of their Korean educational perspective for their children, however.

6. Is the family planning to live overseas for only a
few years, or forever? As mentioned earlier, the family that
expects to return to Korea has a much greater stake in main-

taining their "Korean-ness," both socially and educationally than the family that has left Korea permanently.

7. Why are the parents sending their children to your school? Is it because there is no Korean-language school in your city? Is it because they want to avoid Korean education? Is it because they want to get their children on the track for a Western university education, preferably at a prestigious university? Is it for the personal benefit of the child and his or her future, or is the child part of an extended family economic plan for the next generation, with this child being labeled and chosen already to fill a particular role in the family business? Is it because friends said they should send their children to your school?

By answering these questions you can understand more fully that each child is an individual — a product of birth, of conscious parental decisions, of perhaps capricious decisions of a company or government or mission board, or of sometimes unintentional decisions made by parents. Each family and its history is unique, as is each child's. Past experiences have molded them into the families we meet and the children we see in our classrooms each day. They are special and unique families and children, and deserve to be treated as such.

LOOKING BACK, LOOKING AHEAD

At the beginning of this book you were asked to jot down some characteristics that you personally attributed to ethnic Korean children. You were asked to be honest with yourself, noting both positive and negative characteristics, and to jot down a few questions you might have about these children. Before we go on to discuss how we might be able to make the Western educational experience a positive one for them, look back to see if some of the characteristics you noted earlier make more sense now, if only partially. Think about what you have read regarding the historical, cultural, and educational backdrops sketched here. Consider the individual life experiences of some of the children in your classroom or school. Are things starting to make sense? Are some as confusing as ever? Have some of your questions been answered? Do you have new ones? How could you get the answers?

FROM THE RETURNEES THEMSELVES . . .

"In Korean school the kids pressure you. They compete so much. Competition is the word. Competition comes first. Everyone studies so much. When you are among them, you want to study too, because you don't want it to seem like you are just playing around. Everyone just competes so much. Some kids compete because of their parents, some compete just because they want to be number one. . . When I was in Korean school, I was competitive too. The teachers show favoritism to certain students. I tried very hard, but sometimes I just sat there like a dummy. In the beginning the teachers paid little attention to me. But after a couple of weeks, they started to treat me like the other kids in the class." (Noh, p. 103)

"In America, the reading classes are divided into three different groups. You can study at your own level. You can't do that in Korea. With sixty people, what can you do? Everyone learns the same thing. For smart people it's too easy, and they get bored. For other people it's too hard, and they can't catch up. In America, math was so easy. But here it's so hard. . . In America, the teacher explains everything first, and then asks the students to solve the problems. And while they do the work, she watches them. But here, the teacher does everything. At first school was so hard that I didn't want to go. But now it's OK. It took a few months for me to get used to it. I had to go to school even if I hated it. So I just got up and went." (Noh, p. 104)

"I remember how in Korea I played with dolls and jacks. There's not much different between the way children play in Korea and in the United States. But when you grow up in Korea, all you do is study. The kids have nothing. They just study, study, study. The kids can't hang around hamburger places. They can't have parties. They can't sleep over at their friends' houses. They can't see too many movies; there are many movies they're not allowed to see. There's no place to go but school." (Noh, p. 112)

PART II:

WHERE DO WE GO FROM HERE?

PRACTICAL SUGGESTIONS FOR WORKING WITH ETHNIC KOREAN PARENTS AND THEIR CHILDREN

CHAPTER VII:

WORKING WITH ETHNIC KOREAN PARENTS

Now that we've looked at the background of our Korean parents, it may be helpful to look at some ways in which we can better work with them. Below are some practical suggestions that may be of help.

1. Build the teacher/parent relationship. All human contacts in Korean culture are based on some type of relationship, be it positive or negative. Sitting down to a conference and "getting right down to business" without some "getting to know you as a person" time will be offensive or uncomfortable for many Koreans. When meeting parents, especially for the first time, exchange name cards if you have them (they will); look at their name card and acknowledge the company or organizational connection. (No mention of the position is necessary.) Spend some time talking about the family. Show an interest. Ask about their move. Remembering some of the

93

things you have read about, ask some questions to try to see what this family is all about. Ask about the child. Find out where they are from. Where do they consider "home"? What language is spoken at home? Tell about yourself and where you were educated. Are you married? Do you have children? When did you move to your present location? Where are you from? Let them know you know something about Korea. They will be much more likely to share their ideas and feelings after a few minutes of small talk, finding a few things in common, or sharing a cup of coffee to establish a relationship. Things go much more smoothly after that, and it is time well spent.

2. *Beware of the word "yes".* In talking with native Korean speakers, remember that "Yes" does not necessarily mean agreement, but only indicates understanding. Much as in English we might say "uh-huh" to indicate that we are following the conversation and understand the speaker, in Korean one uses the same word as for "yes." When this is translated into English, it comes out "yes" instead of "I see," or "Uh-huh." (Western business people have sat through days of apparently agreeable negotiations punctuated with "yes's" only to realize, as the deal was about to be clinched, that nothing at all had been agreed to!) In addition, in the interest of maintaining harmony, a parent might not say "no" outright, but would hint around it. (A hint of disagreement could often be if the parent said that something would be "really difficult." That usually means "no.") Try to be aware of such a gentle "no." Don't be afraid to ask for clarification. Another frequent source of misunderstanding is that in Korean, negative questions are answered by "Yes, I agree" or "No, I don't agree." For example, if you ask, "Your child doesn't speak English, does she?" the parent might answer

"Yes," which in this case means "Yes, you're correct, she doesn't speak English." Conversely, a "No" answer would mean, "No, you're mistaken, my child *does* speak English." This confusion can be avoided by simply asking only positive questions — "Does your daughter speak English?" — for simple "Yes" or "No" answers.

3. Find ways to help Korean parents understand the Western philosophy of your school. Taejon Christian International School in Korea has published an excellent pamphlet entitled "Understanding a Western Education." (See list of resources.) This pamphlet, printed in both English and Korean, describes Western educational approaches important to the school such as teaching the "whole" child, encouraging the development and use of higher thinking skills beyond memorization of facts, involving parents in the educational process, the handling of discipline with an eye towards fairness and consistency, placing a realistic emphasis on grades, the utilization of a variety of assessment tools (beyond pencil and paper tests), emphasizing realistic college selection, and using English both in and out of the classroom. Various schools may find different areas of misunderstanding or even conflict with parents, and may wish to develop such a pamphlet of their own, being sure to have it translated into Korean by someone with a strong understanding of both the school and Western education. To that end, you might help ethnic Korean parents understand some of the differences between Korean and Western education, such as those that follow.

a) *the competition of the individual against him or herself rather than against classmates.* In most Western nations, there is space enough in higher education for any student who has the academic credentials and the desire to attend college. While not everyone can get into the most prestigious schools, few who truly aspire to higher education go uneducated if they are willing to work for it. Therefore, the emphasis is on doing one's best, discovering and developing one's individual talents, and setting realistic goals rather than competing against peers and being number one in the class. For parents who might have only experienced the intensely competitive Korean educational system, this is often difficult to understand and might even be interpreted as encouraging laziness or a lack of ambition. Conversely, a student with little competitive spirit who returns to a Korean school will be severely handicapped.

b) *the development of a well-rounded student.* Whereas in Korean education expertise in the arts or sports is given a nod, for most "good" students *academics* is all important. Korean schools do not generally have sports teams (unless they are special sports high schools), bands, or other such extracurricular activities. While a rich club program is emphasized at the middle school level, usually these clubs all meet at the same time on specific afternoons each month. In high school they are noticeably absent, and would certainly not affect college admissions decisions. For children whose educational future lies in North America, parents need to understand that "straight A's" and an SAT score of 1600 won't get Kyung Min into Harvard; top schools want more than just a bookworm. Unfortunately, parents often hear this to mean that Kyung Min must also be captain of the basketball team, sit first chair violin in the school orchestra, be president of the Student Council, *and* get the "A's"! On the other hand, if the student is returning to Korea, we must realize that while all these activities might make the child a much better person, it generally won't help him get into Seoul National. Possibly in this case the most realistic long-term solution would be to let Kyung Min keep his nose in the books. It might be against our educational philosophy, but where he is going our philosophy, while popular in theory, is not yet reality.

c) *the use of a developmentally appropriate curriculum.* In a highly competitive system, the student who goes the fastest and farthest wins the race. In a system that emphasizes memorization to the detriment of understanding, expertise over the development of creativity, and acceptance of the "right answer" before the development of a critical mind, this often translates into a dependence on memorization. For example, it is no secret that Korean (and often Japanese) children far outpace children from the United States on standardized math tests in high school. By high school, they may be years ahead of their Western counterparts. However, if we accept Piagetian theory and research in cognitive development (as well as our own experience), we know, for example, that it is not possible for most middle schoolers to *understand* higher-level algebra. Yes, they can memorize formulas and theorems and apply them to specific types of problems, but real understanding in depth is beyond all but a few. Students can sometimes be pushed, step-by-step and chapter-by-chapter, beyond what would appear to be their ability, and they may even earn good grades. However, most often a review a year later will show that there has been little retention, even for very talented students. It makes sense that such pressure to advance rapidly would be effective in a system where memorization, a very low level thinking skill, is used and valued so widely. The fact that higher level thinking skills are stressed in Western education, and that these thinking skills also in large part dependent upon natural cognitive development, needs to be impressed upon parents who may be thinking in terms only of learning (memorizing) more and more information rather than developing higher level skills such as analysis, evaluation, and application. Conversely, while we may decry the force feeding of higher level math upon upper elementary students, if they are planning on returning to Korea they must learn (that is, memorize) this material if they are not to fall far behind. Whether or not your school allows this is a philosophical question worth some serious discussion and soul-searching. Don't worry that you are setting your students up for failure if you refuse to put fifth graders in high school algebra classes, though! Parents may, and often do, subscribe to monthly home study practice and advanced math programs called *"kong-mun-su-hak"* that keep students abreast, and sometimes ahead of, their peers at home. Such programs are widely used in Korea. They are most likely already in use by many of your students. You may be interested in seeing some of the materials they are using. Don't be afraid to ask to see them.

d) the importance of cultural diversity. Interestingly, this is one of the most difficult challenges facing schools anywhere that have a large number of ethnic Korean students. A national history of persecution, a strong group identity, and a shared experience makes them, to a degree somewhat beyond that of many other ethnic groups, stick together in groups and exclude others. While not necessarily "gangs" in the traditional sense, the sense of group loyalty and nationalism is often strong. (Evidence of this might be to find the graffiti "K.P." scrawled on the walls of the rest rooms; it means "Korean Power.") This phenomenon is found on college campuses in the United States, in public and private schools outside of Korea among first and second-generation immigrants, and in international schools in Korea and elsewhere.

This strong collective sense seems very natural to Korean parents. While they may have chosen to send their child to your school to learn English, to rub elbows with Western children, and to learn Western ways, they do not understand that the experience of living outside of Korea or attending international schools in Korea will necessarily make their children less than 100% Korean. When parents see this starting to happen, they may steer their children into choosing only ethnic Korean friends. Seldom is this verbally expressed, but it is there nonetheless. Often, it is just based on parental fear of the unknown. Parents need to know that the school is consciously working to have students mix with and learn from each other both academically and socially, and that you actively encourage mixing among national and/or ethnic groups. Normally, this is not much of an issue in elementary school, but as the children get older, usually between grades six and eight, the ethnic separation begins. Parents may get particularly involved at the high school level if and when inter-racial dating begins. They may react by forbidding their children (particularly daughters) to date at all or if they do, to date only other ethnic Koreans. Possibly fear of Western morality (or lack thereof) is often the real issue. Frequently other Korean students will ostracize anyone who dates outside their group, and a non-Korean interloper trying to date a Korean may be scared off. The fact is that even today in Korea, marrying a non-Korean often causes severe family strife and rejection. Biracial children who attend Korean schools are still the victims of taunts and name-calling. Such attitudes are both the root and the result of this kind of prejudice. Such preferences may be considered to be simply signs of a healthy ethnic identity, but when stripped of their Korean-ness they would be more accurately termed racial prejudice and xenophobia. Additionally, it is a sad fact that while romantic contact between Korean and Caucasian young people is often strongly frowned upon and may bring shame on the family, such contact with students of African heritage is often truly abhorred. Koreans have unfortunately had little contact with people of color, and that which they have had is mostly limited to twenty-year-old American GI's posted far from home.

e) that education is a process, not a performance. Korean parents tend to see a report card as a final sentence, a blot (or star) on the future. That children are "not done yet," that their children are dealing with a lot more in their lives than formal education, and that a grade report is a milestone rather than a finish line, must be repeatedly stressed. "Yes, Soo-young had a difficult job on her research project on dinosaurs, but she learned a lot from her mistakes" will be heard but not understood. That fact that Soo-young earned a "C" on the project might instead result in demands for extended homework hours, the hiring of a tutor, dad helping just a little too much on the next project (to ensure a good grade) or even physical punishment. The grade is seen, quite simply, as being more important than the learning that has gone into it. It is a true "mark" on the person and their future, as well as on the family. In Korean education, that unfortunately is all too often true.

If it is expected that the child has some type of legitimate learning difficulty, this will have to be explained to parents very carefully. Learning differences, A.D.D., and A.D.H.D. are not at all well known or understood. Difficulties in school are almost always looked upon as ability or motivational problems: Min-ju is either stupid or lazy. Even if the parents can be made to understand the nature of the problem, they may refuse treatment or even diagnostic testing due to fear of possible social stigma. Should testing not be available in your city, it *is* available on a limited basis in Seoul, where it can be administered in Korean. You may have to insist on such testing as a condition of enrollment. Insist on have the results translated and signed by the doctor and a copy sent directly to you.

4. *Watch out for excessive pressure from home.* For reasons that should now be apparent, parents may apply very strong pressure on their children to do exceptionally well in school. One result of this is the extreme academic competition that often rages among students and their mothers. Korean culture by nature is a competitive one. Any posted honor roll list will attract immediate attention, and you may find out that some of the moms are more aware of who is on the honor roll (and who is not) than the counselor is. Comparisons among parents of their children's standardized test results, college acceptances, S.A.T. scores, and report card grades are common.

Parental demands that a child be placed in a grade or level ahead of where the school may feel is appropriate may also occur. Note that as the Korean school year ends in February (actual effective instruction ends in December, followed by a long vacation before advancement to the next grade) admissions personnel in Western-style schools following a Northern Hemisphere calendar will have to decide whether to put the child "ahead" a semester or keep them back and have them repeat part of the same grade. Parents will be very anxious that their

Comparisons among parents of their children's standardized test results, college acceptances, S.A.T. scores, and report card grades are common.

child will "be behind his peers a year when he goes back to Korea" if he or she has to repeat a half year in your school. This is true, and if they are going to return within year or two, it is probably better to let them have their way. Otherwise, the child may be truly ostracized when he returns. However, if the family plans to stay overseas or be in your school any longer than that, particularly if E.S.L. help is necessary, do not be afraid to insist that the child repeat half a year. For example, if a child entering your school in February or March has just completed Grade 6 in Korean school, placing the student in Grade 6 and having him or her "repeat" the end of the year is probably preferable to having them skip half a year by placing them midway through Grade 7. Conversely, remember that a child entering in August or September will have only completed half of the school year back in Korea. Don't be afraid to stand up to parents' pleas to put the child ahead. They may not have any appreciation or understanding of the social, academic, and linguistic challenges that lie ahead for their child, although they know the child will have to "study hard."

There may also be excessive pressure on the school to place a child inappropriately in an advanced section of a class. It takes a strong and principled teacher or counselor to stand up to such pressure, especially if it is accompanied by a graciously given gift or an enjoyable evening out at a restaurant. Any special favor given to one family certainly be followed by similar ones from other friends.

Parents may, as mentioned earlier, give too much help with homework or projects, not in any attempt to cheat, but just because a good grade is so important to them. Extra tutors may be hired unbeknownst to the school. Expectations for college acceptances at only the very "best" colleges may be placed on students, and many children from prominent families may even have their future role in the extended family business mapped out for them in elementary school. Counselors need to be aware of this, whether or not they agree to such practices.

Students may be shamed by their parents or even physically punished for less than perfect grades; more than one middle or high school student has been seen dissolving

103

into tears on report card day because of the expected reaction at home to the one "A-" which mars an otherwise perfect report card. That fear may or may not be well founded. Other common punishments are being told to sit outside on the steps all night (later let in by the other parent), being given the "silent treatment" for days by a parent, or having the threat of "I'll send you to Korean school" hang over heads. Korean parents can be brutal in shaming their children: "Die!", "You don't deserve to be my son!" or "Fool!" are common angry comments. The love is deep, though, and the child knows that the parent really doesn't mean it. Often, the one most upset is the Western teacher who is within earshot!

5. *Help parents understand what is acceptable Western social behavior.* Remember that these parents grew up in a turbulent, but very socially protected Korea in the 1950's and 60's. In their childhood days drugs were the toys of organized crime; tobacco was used only by adult men and elderly women, and drinking was strictly limited to college and beyond. Boys and girls were strictly separated until college, attending segregated middle and high schools. Sexual contact among young people was almost unknown, except for maybe among high school dropouts who worked in factories. Parents may not realize that these attractive dangers are very available to their children and to their children's peers, depending on where they live. Furthermore, parents may not be aware of or have their parental radar turned on for signs of social problems. A few strange smelling leaves in a bureau drawer will be assumed to have come off In-Young's socks; alcohol on the breath can readily be excused away as mouthwash, and stale cigarette smell on clothes can be blamed on a taxi driver. While we don't want to alarm parents unneces-

sarily, we do owe it to them to let them know gently if we see their son or daughter showing signs of anti-social or self-destructive behavior that parents might simply think is a result of normal acculturation. On the other hand, Korea is one of the most wired and Internet-savvy nations in the world. Although they may have an unrealistically high regard for their child's social naiveté, they are well aware of the darker corners of the Internet and all it has to offer inquisitive young minds.

6. *Understand that parents may keep their children dependent on them well into adulthood, and help them understand how difficult this dependency may make it for their children to succeed on their own in a Western university.* Korean students are supposed to be just that — students. They are not supposed to have to worry about other time-consuming duties. Thus, Korean children generally do not have chores to do around the house, even making their own bed or taking their dishes to the sink. Teachers might be surprised to find that their middle or even high school Korean students have never washed a dish, made a bed, or thrown a load of clothes in the wash. It's not that it is below them, they simply don't know how. Mom does these things; the child is to spend his or her time with the nose in the books. While this does not cause any particular difficulty for the school, it can cause a great deal of difficulty for the child when he or she goes off to boarding school or college. Simple survival skills are often missing. In addition, children may have never had to work for money, and may be given a generous allowance with no responsibilities attached. Even after students have gone off to North America or Europe to university, more than a few Korea mothers "commute" every month or so to check up on their son or daughter, clean their room, make

105

A TRUE STORY

Mee-jung was one of the smartest girls in her prestigious private Korean elementary school in Seoul, and was at the top of her class. Her mother, a woman of culture and intelligence, hired an English-speaking Korean woman married to an American teacher to tutor her daughter with the goal of eventually gaining entrance to a private American boarding school. Mee-jung studied hard and stayed at the top of her class throughout middle school. Eventually, the tutor and her husband were able to get her into a very prestigious New England boarding school for ninth grade. Unfortunately, what Mee-jung had in intelligence she lacked in common sense and independence. Her life had been so totally organized for her (violin and piano lessons, art lessons, English lessons, etc., etc.) that she didn't know how to wash her clothes, cook a bowl of ramyon, or pick up after herself. More crucial, she didn't have the self-discipline to organize her own time or get herself up in the morning, and quickly was in academic difficulty. Within two years she and her mother were searching for another school. Eventually she returned to Korea, her American education a failure not due to any academic limitations or even English language difficulties, but to a dismal lack of self-motivation, independence, survival skills, and common sense. By being everything a good Korean student should be she never developed the abilities necessary to fulfill her parents' dream for her of an American prep school and college education. More to the point, her mother, by being everything a good Korean mother should be, raised a daughter so dependent and lacking in maturity that she simply could not survive in an American educational and social environment, where independence and self-direction are demanded.

some Korean food, and generally be sure that Choon-ho is being taken care of. Boys in particular may be considered to be in need of a mother's attention.

Another example of prolonged dependence, noted earlier, is the tendency for parents (either mother or father) to "take responsibility" for their children's actions. "It's my fault, don't blame him" is all too often heard when a Korean child gets in trouble. You can be sure that justice will be meted out at home (the family has been embarrassed, after all) but any type of punishment that may be found out by other parents is avoided at all costs. Administrators need to assure parents that just because Yung-jin is being suspended for two days, you will not publicize it. They may well ask if this incident will be recorded "in his record' and beg that it not be. There is a good deal of public shame suffered by the parents when a child gets in trouble. It takes backbone to stand up to pleas to not discipline Yung-jin this time in return for a promise from his parents that it won't happen again. Don't except the excuse that he didn't know any better, and that it is just the result of bad parenting. That may well be, but Yung-jin still has to be disciplined!

Parents may also try to take responsibility for a child's academic success or failure by promising better grades or greater success in the future. The chance of retention or probation may be perceived as a family shame rather than any shortcoming on the part of the child. Again, while the child will bear the full brunt of the responsibility when he or she gets home, parents will want to avoid any chance that other parents will find out about the problem.

We can help parents by explaining that although we all want their children to do as well as they can in school, by pampering them, by not allowing them to fail once in a while (and thus learn that it is they, not the parents, who "own" the grades), by making life too easy, and by making excuses they are raising children so dependent on them that they will have a very difficult time surviving on their own in a Western college or university where personal self-survival skills are so important. Baring such support, to succeed in university outside of Korea students need to be much more than great students – they need to become independent people able and willing to take care of themselves.

7. *Understand that in the parents' eyes, academic success or failure is tantamount to success or failure as a valuable person.* This idea is well expressed by the authors of *Handbook for Teaching Korean-American Students*, p. 29, (1992) published by the Bilingual Education Office of the California Department of Education. I will share those observations here:

"Parents in Korea generally support the schools and hope for fulfillment of their own lives through the success of their children. Parents instill in their children very early the idea that parental acceptance is contingent on high performance in school. The Korean community as well as family and relatives often give prominence to and recognize high academic performance. When the report card is sent to parents, they often call each other to compare their children's grades, knowledge of which is shared by parents, relatives, and neighbors. Korean children feel obligated to receive high grades and are imbued with the notion that their academic success is linked to the family's reputation. Students learn early that they are working not merely for themselves but for their family as well. Keenly concerned about their performance, they become competitive not only for their own sake but also for their family's prestige. Low performance levels elicit parental disapproval, criticism, disappointment, and sometimes shame among relatives and friends."

8. *Parents may look to you for advice and help; they see you in partnership raising their kids. Don't hold back.* Korean parents are often not the ones who administer discipline to their own children. Quite often the school is expected to provide this. Parents can and do threaten their children that they will report bad behavior to the teacher (a 180-degree switch from what many of us are used to!) When a child gets into trouble on the streets, the police often contact the school before contacting the parents. Korean schools have at least one faculty member on duty 24 hours a day, seven days a week, for just such emergencies. Teachers are expected to play an active role in the moral upbringing of their students beyond the walls of the classroom. Therefore, do not be hesitant to counsel parents and help them in cross-cultural situations. They will be truly grateful for your help and insight. While they may not take all of your advice, you can be sure that as an educator you are possibly more highly regarded socially than you regard yourself; the very honorable status of teachers in Korea will most likely be applied to you. This status is based on your education, morality and leadership. You may be approached for child-rearing guidance, especially in matters related to school or acculturation. If you feel confident in this area, don't be afraid to offer help. Remember, however, that in their eyes you are still a foreigner. In really important matters, family friends, and especially older extended family members who may have very little understanding of a Western-style school situation, are also very influential.

9. *Understand that while at school you see a bicultural, or even totally Westernized child, parents may see a 100% Korean child at home. They may not recognize that their child is not totally Korean any more.* It was mentioned

earlier that generally Koreans' sense of national identity and "groupness" often make it difficult for them to see shades of Korean-ness or recognize and appreciate biculturalism. While they will readily acknowledge that their child now is fluent in English, or now wears different clothes, or has different tastes in food, they still quite naturally still think of their child as being really Korean rather than bicultural or a TCK. Helping them to understand this sometimes causes some degree of regret or guilt on the part of the parents, but it may well help parents to understand their children better, and vice-versa.

10. Understand that many ethnic Korean parents may see themselves as outsiders from the Western school culture. This author, even after living in Korea for more than twenty-five years, is still considered an "outsider." The Korean word for "foreigner" is "a person from outside"; this is not just a linguistic form but reflects a real perception. An overseas ethnic Korean, then, may naturally expect that he or she is considered an outsider by host country nationals or by the Western school community. Sensitivity to this perception, and a conscious effort to include ethnic Korean parents in school events and activities, is welcome and helpful. Help them get involved in the PTA, ask them to be room mothers, or find some committees on which they can serve. They want very much to be involved, and can and will be a really positive, involved, and hard-working force in your school. Just ask them to put on a Korean meal and get ready to enjoy a feast!

11. Don't misinterpret non-involvement by parents as a lack of interest in their children. Koreans are very proud of their children — after all, they are the future of the extended family. Fathers tend not to be involved in their education but may have a much better command of English than the mothers do. In a Western school this thrusts the dads into a new role — that of the school contact — in which they might feel quite uncomfortable. Mothers, on the other hand, may be embarrassed about their lack of English language ability, be hesitant to admit that they are having difficulties with their children, lack understanding about what their role is in the school, or simply fear the unknown. Actually, their English is often much better than they believe it to be, but a natural humility often prevents them from admitting it. If they seem hesitant to attend parent conferences, invite them to bring along a friend to interpret. Teachers should not be afraid to make contact and invite *both* parents to school. It may be necessary to *insist* on the father's attendance at conferences if you suspect that the child's mother isn't handling a situation effectively. Because the mother can sometimes "get in trouble" herself from her husband if the children don't do well, sometimes the father does not find out about difficulties until too late. Try to include him in discussions before things reach a critical stage either academically or socially.

12. Help parents network with each other. While this often happens very naturally without school help, a newly arrived family needs the security of talking to others who have had the same experience. If this network can be brought to work *for* instead of *against* the school, all the better. If possible, administrators should maintain contact with some of the leaders (both fathers and mothers) in the school's Korean community. Other families will look to them for advice and leadership. It is advantageous for these leaders to understand your school, your priorities and your programs rather than for the community to react to the latest rumor or tidbit of news. Otherwise, you may find that some of your work is be-

Monthly email?

111

ing unwittingly sabotaged from outside without your knowledge, due only to a lack of understanding and information. Some schools have employed a bi-lingual and bi-cultural "Korean Community Liaison" to be an on-call translator of both language and culture, and to organize activities that enhance the relationship between the Korean and Western communities. This has been appreciated by both communities.

13. *Decide ahead of time how to handle the "gift problem.* Korean culture demands that gifts be used to cement relationships — and the parent-teacher relationship is no exception. Gifts sometimes tend to be expensive, and may come in "white envelopes" (rather generous gifts of cash). This is not to be confused with a bribe for good grades (which seldom happens), but is rather a way of saying "I appreciate the care you show for my child. Please keep it up." Bribes are not unknown in Korean society, however, and one would be wise to be conscious not only of the possibly that the real intent of a gift is not so harmless, but also of the outward appearance of accepting something less than a token of simple thanks. This is especially important to keep in mind for those with admissions responsibilities or those who write college recommendations. The size of the gift often depends on the finances and social status of the family. While the business family may be quite generous, a missionary may feel comfortable with a more modest gift of food or note of thanks.

Most gifts are just that — gifts. If they are excessive in value, however, a teacher or administrator may feel obliged to return them. This can be very difficult, and it is not only uncomfortable for the educator but is truly horrifying and humiliating for the parent. A gift returned is really a slap in the face to the giver. It is better to have a school "Gift Limit Policy" which is publicized widely among teachers and parents.

This will take administrative support, and will inevitably cause some embarrassment for both parents and school. One school handles this by requiring that teachers give all gifts over a certain value ($100???) to their administrator, who will accept the gift with thanks "in the name of the school." Cash might be put into a student activity fund and "real" gifts held for the annual faculty party door prizes. If a gift policy is widely known and followed, the word will soon get out that while a meal out or a box of Korean rice cakes is appreciated, an expensive watch or an envelope of cash puts the teacher in a truly awkward spot. As can be imagined, this can be a sticky problem requiring tact and courage on everyone's part.

If you receive a gift, correct etiquette is to act slightly embarrassed and protest, and then take the gift gently with both hands and quietly put it aside unless asked to open it, and thank the giver. Normally, gifts are not opened in the presence of the giver, as the giver will be embarrassed at the "small size and worthlessness of such a gift."

14. **Learn something about Korean culture and help others in your school do the same.** This will greatly strengthen relationships between the school and the home. Never assume that they are just like Japanese or Chinese parents. Although there are many similarities from a Western perspective, there are some real and important differences, as well, not the least of which is a deep-seated distrust of the Japanese by some older Koreans due to lingering memories of the colonial occupation. There also exists a reciprocal superiority by many Japanese towards their "uncultured" Korean neighbors across the sea to the west, whom they call "garlic eaters." Taking the time to learn a few words of Korean (see the back of this book) will go a long way towards establishing a positive working relationship with parents. Learn about

Korea and its culture by going beyond the encyclopedia and "war stories" of former soldiers (see the annotated bibliography at the back of this book). Korea has a rich, long, and fascinating history and a culture of which it is justly proud. It is a modern, vibrant, cultured, and exciting nation. Your interest in Korea will greatly enhance your credibility. The local Korean consulate or embassy should have some materials for you to borrow or keep, and <amazon.com> is a handy resource, as well. Your interest and knowledge will be not be expected, but will be greatly appreciated. If you are invited into a Korean home, gladly accept. You will have a terrific meal and will be treated like royalty. Don't be surprised if mom spends most of the time in the kitchen, though, and remember to take your shoes off at the door! Taking a bouquet of flowers as a gift is appropriate, if you wish, as is any home-made baked good. If you are invited out, be sure to clarify whether or not your spouse is also included, as often in Korea they are not. You'll probably never be considered a member of the family, but take advantage of any opportunity you have to learn more about Korea and the families you serve.

LOOKING BACK, LOOKING AHEAD

What difficult situations have you experienced with Korean parents that now make more sense? Knowing what you know now, how might you handled it differently?

What might your school do to better serve Korean parents? How is your school communicating with them? It is working?

How can your school accommodate the needs and demands of Korean parents while remaining true to the goals and philosophy of the school? How might you better communicate these goals to Korean parents?

Where can you learn more about Korea and Koreans? How could you share that with your co-workers?

If Koreans are a large portion of your student body, what is your school doing to enhance understanding of Korean students and parents by your teachers?

CHAPTER VIII:

WORKING WITH ETHNIC KOREAN STUDENTS

Korean students, unless they are coming directly from Korea or have always lived there, will generally be "less Korean" than their parents. Therefore, this section should be approached with even more care than the previous one lest unfair and inaccurate generalizations be made.

1.   For Korean-speaking E.S.L. students, be aware that initial class placements may seriously affect whether or not a child progresses appropriately. This suggestion is directed at school personnel who actually make class assignments for E.S.L. students.

Western education often equates superior teachers with those who are innovative, who provide an active classroom atmosphere full of spontaneity, and who plan lessons full of student-led activities and interaction. Certainly teachers like these are among the best. However, the very qualities that stimulate and excite and inspire the native speaking student can confuse, upset, disorient, and actually hinder positive school adjustment and English acquisition for any new E.S.L. student, whatever his or her native language. This is true for two reasons. First, at least during the initial stages of language acquisition, an orderly and routine environment provides the psychologically safe, secure, and predictable environment necessary for learning. New E.S.L. students very often find it easier to learn in classrooms that have a greater sense of organization and routine, in which the instruction is more teacher-centered, and in which instructions and assignments are clear and unambiguous.   A second reason that careful class placement is important pertains particularly to students who are coming from an educational system such as Korea's in which students do not speak unless spoken to and which emphasizes a rigid and formal educational atmosphere. They may become very uncomfortable in the looser environment found in many Western classrooms.   Korean students are not alone. Children coming from French or Japanese schools, for example, are often unsettled by the comparative lack of apparent structure found in many U.S. style classrooms. First year placement for any E. S. L. student, and particularly for those from such countries, is best in traditional classrooms where there is a regular routine, clear classroom rules, strong organization, and a generally quiet and businesslike atmosphere.

2. *Avoid putting too many Korean children in one class (especially if they speak Korean).* The natural tendency of any group of children (or adults) of any nationality when there are more than four or five in a class is to begin to segregate themselves socially.   One of the most commonly reported social issues concerning Korean children, who already share a strong sense of ethnicity and group consciousness, is that they often tend to isolate themselves from students of other backgrounds.   This can happen within an elementary school classroom, but to an even greater extent in upper middle and high school, where cliques may easily form. Experienced teachers see it begin to take hold in Grade 6 and come to full flower in Grades 8 and 9. Some schools have found very little difficulty with such self-imposed social segregation by their ethnic Korean students; others struggle with it con-

stantly as it has a strong influence on extracurricular activities, class elections, and other social and affective aspects of school life.

What can the school do about this? There is little that can be done to ensure ethnic mixing in the lunchroom or at a dance, but attempts should be made in the classroom to consciously mix students as much as possible in work groups. Activities that encourage ethnic mixing, particularly sports, should be encouraged. Two of the greatest integrative forces among students of different ethnic backgrounds are the basketball court and soccer field.

Another negative result of such a strong group identity is that of students covering up for each other in times of trouble. Korean young people are not alone in this, of course, but the solidarity with which they may refuse to "tell on" a friend is often surprising to the Westerner. Often, one older student may "take responsibility" for the misdeeds of other younger students in the group, but refuse to identify them. This is similar to what happens in Korea when a building collapses or a train goes off the track. As long as a high-level officer (often a government minister) resigns in shame, his taking "moral" responsibility (even if it was clearly not his fault) satisfies the community that the matter has been dealt with and punishment meted out – someone has been blamed and shamed. Korean students may expect you to treat them the same way.

3. *De-emphasize memorization; encourage thinking and understanding.* Children who have come directly from Korean school often tend to do very well on tasks that require memorization (remember that the historical basis for Korean education is the memorization of Chinese characters). Parents will encourage that type of learning. However, an as-

118

signment demanding thoughtful, creative answers at a higher level of thinking can often create something close to panic. Students have been trained to find the one right answer coming from some higher authority, usually either the book or the teacher. If faced suddenly with a "What do you think, and why?" question, the student may be genuinely confused. They need to be taught to expect such questions, and must learn how to develop and express their own opinions without fear of reprisal. The use of thought-provoking essay questions on tests for which there is no "right" answer, discussions in class which demand individual expression of opinions, writing assignments requiring higher thinking skills, and an atmosphere in which it is safe to take intellectual risks without fear of being "wrong" are crucial.

While language learning is very important in Korean education, writing anything more than a paragraph or two is uncommon (in part due to class size). Learning to write extended written assignments and developing formal English speaking skills is very important.

On the other hand, in Korean elementary schools "summer vacation projects" are often assigned. Unfortunately, in a competitive system where a good deal of public comparison takes place, parental input may be somewhat higher than is acceptable in Western education. If a project looks too good to be true, it might be smart to ask some questions about how, who, and when the project was done.

4. *Encourage students to ask questions*. Generally, in Korean school students are not encouraged to ask questions. There may be two reasons for this. One is that with large class sizes, it is simply too disruptive to have individuals ask questions. The second reason is rooted in the Confucian-based idea that the teacher is the font of all knowledge. Cer-

119

tainly to challenge that academic authority by disagreeing with the teacher is very difficult for a student to do. In addition, by asking a question, the student may feel that he or she is implying that the teacher didn't do a very good job of explaining (lecturing) in the first place. This could be interpreted as being rude or disrespectful. Finally, the student might be afraid to let the teacher know that he or she doesn't understand the material. Therefore, be sure that students are encouraged (even required) not only to ask questions in class, but to see the teacher after school for extra help, if that is appropriate. There is a strong tendency among Korean parents to rely on paid, after school tutors rather than on the child's teachers. While parents of course work hard to get the best tutors possible for their children, sometimes these tutors have little or no qualifications save having been a "former Harvard student." The fact that this person might not be a native English speaker, may have few teaching skills, or may have no interest in young people may be mitigated by the professed "Harvard" pedigree. Depending on tutors is a difficult habit to break. Be sure your parents know what extra help is available at school, and when. One teacher requires students who seem hesitant to be involved to ask at least one question each class period and lets them know that their grade will depend on it. While using grades as a motivation may rub some of us the wrong way, it might be that focusing on grades may be the most effective lever you have with both students and parents. However, both students and parents need to understand that grades depend on more than just memorizing facts, listening to the teacher lecture, and spewing information back on an exam. Students need permission and encouragement to ask questions, to challenge the teacher, and to take an active and contributing role in the class.

5. *Be sure the girls don't get ignored.* In a Confucian society such as Korea's females are taught, either overtly or by example, to defer to males, at least outside of the home. Both legally and socially, women are still greatly discriminated against in Korea, although there has been great improvement in this area in the past twenty years. Generally, women work in low-status jobs (bank teller, office worker, waitress) or just stay at home until they get married. Married women do not normally work unless they are teachers, nurses, or doctors. The legal profession, the business world, the clergy, and the medical profession (except nurses) are overwhelmingly male, although not at all closed to women. Particularly when a woman becomes pregnant, she is expected (by society, by the family, and by the company) to resign her position. Staying home, raising children (preferably sons), and being a good wife, mother, and daughter-in-law are still very strong expectations for women in Korean society. Girls thus learn to defer to males and develop the role of being quiet and subservient, particularly in public.

In addition, many girls coming directly from Korean middle or high schools may have been in single-sex schools, which are still very common. Being with boys may embarrass and frighten them. Thus, in the classroom many ethnic Korean girls may tend to "disappear." Certainly this phenomenon is not limited to Korean girls, but they tend to exhibit this behavior to a greater extent than more Westernized girls might. Therefore, it is imperative for the teacher to direct questions to girls, to actively engage the girls in class discussion, and to praise their involvement. Be sure the boys don't dominate them, either.

6. *Understand and confront issues of academic integrity.* This is a delicate topic, open to a good deal of debate.

121

However, it is also a matter of much discussion among teachers of ethnic Korean students, at least those who teach in international schools in Korea. Certainly cheating is found among students of all backgrounds, but the reasons behind this occurring and the types of individuals involved may be somewhat particular to Korean students.

Extreme academic pressure from home, friends, or one's self, coupled with intense loyalty to friends and "the group" are most often the cause of dishonesty among ethnic Korean students. Not letting a friend copy homework or not telling what was on last period's test is even harder for a Korean child than for many Western children. This is complicated by the fact that while the school may classify copying homework or glancing over a neighbor's test paper as dishonesty, in the Korean context it may be considered to be cooperation, helping a friend, or just doing what is necessary to succeed in what is perceived as a highly competitive environment. Students also speak of being under so much pressure to be at the top of the class that they are "forced" to cheat — that there are few other ways to succeed. Quite simply, academic success, when push comes to shove, sometimes takes on a higher value than honesty. "The end justifies the means" to a greater extent than we are usually comfortable with in the West. In a highly pressured situation *how* the work gets done is not always as important as *getting it done.* When schedules get tight, you may even find parents or tutors helping out by doing homework, as homework is not considered by parents to be practice work but rather a performance that must be correct. Teachers need to make very clear to both parents and students what the expectations *are* regarding homework — how, when, and by whom it should be done. The difference between "getting help" and copying work needs to be explained unambiguously. Teachers should be clear: "This project should be done by working in pairs," or "This is not a group exercise. Everyone should be working on their own. I want to see what you can do, not what you and your neighbor can do together." The school would do well to develop a statement on academic integrity, defining what is cheating and what is not, and developing clear and appropriate guidelines for discipline for various infractions. These guidelines should be published in both student and parent handbooks and openly discussed with parents.

A related issue is plagiarism. In Korea, plagiarism and copyright violation is so widespread that even university professors routinely tell students where they can buy pirated copies of foreign texts. (This author was told by a professor from one of the "top" universities in Seoul that she would like to use an earlier version of this book as a text for a course on culture and education. When I asked how many copies they would like, the answer was, "Oh, don't worry, we'll just have them copied for the students.") Lack of instruction in original thinking encourages lots of cutting and pasting from web sites when researching. While this is certainly a problem in other countries as well, in Korea it is quite openly tolerated within academia. Well-educated adults who study in the United States are very surprised at the rules governing citations and copying. Taught to revere and honor those of greater education and wisdom who have gone before, it is almost considered a compliment to copy their words and works, and there is little educational tradition of showing how to cite them. The concept of intellectual property rights is a very new one in Korea and elsewhere in Asia, and seldom receives more than lip service from academia or the government. This is clearly a case of different cultural norms. Certainly a high school student brought up in such an environment of blatant (and acceptable) plagiarism cannot be ex-

123

pected to know the finer points of what constitutes plagiarism. Teachers should be expected to carefully instruct them as to what is acceptable and then follow up, expecting (as with any other new concept) some stumbles along the way. International schools have a unique opportunity to help bring Korea up to international standards in this area through its young people.

One reason teachers are often so shocked by (or blind to) dishonest behavior is that often the students who cheat are the same ones we would trust completely in other situations. They are sincere, respectful, hard-working, high-achieving, and otherwise totally honorable kids. However, the academic pressure is often so strong, and the consequences for poor performance so high, that they give in to the pressure. While they understand that it is wrong, academic success may take precedence. Honesty is certainly an important Korean value, but in the hierarchy of values solidarity with one's group, educational success, and the fear of embarrassing one's family with poor grades may temporarily become a higher priority. You can "hate the sin and love the sinner" in these cases. Be vigilant! Many parents would agree with this assessment of values, but may blame the teacher or the school for being lax by making it easy for kids to cheat. Too often they are right. With Korean students and parents, teachers may be operating with a different set of values and ethics than they are used to. Of course, it should also go without saying that many, if not most, ethnic Korean children and parents abhor cheating in any form — they may just define it differently.

7. Understand the difference between counseling and advising. Cultures that place a very high value on strong family solidarity, often against "outsiders," tend not to react well to Western style counseling (see Sue and Sue), which looks at underlying causes of a problem rather than surface symptoms and practical solutions. If a parent or student from such a culture (some Hispanic groups share this characteristic with many East Asians, including Koreans) comes to a teacher or counselor for help, they are not coming to work through some deep personal or family dysfunction such as divorce, suicide, alcoholism, or abuse that may be causing academic distress. Those serious problems are secrets that are kept safely guarded behind the wall that surrounds the Korean home. Rather than coming for *counseling*, a role that is handled by older relatives, they are probably coming for *advice*. Unfortunately for many of our students overseas, they are not living near older relatives, and because many of the problems they face are cultural ones between parents and children, the children have no one to go to except friends or adults at school. It may take some very direct questioning to even begin to get to the root of a problem. Don't be surprised if you never seem to be able to get to the bottom of a situation — it may be a family difficulty the child just can't and won't discuss. Compounding this problem is that often such difficulties are not discussed at home, either, and the first person to whom a child has really talked about it after suffering for months or even years may be a teacher or counselor. Parents may resent "the school" prying into family matters, but a professional decision must sometimes be made as to what is best for the child. If parents understand that a personal or family problem might be having academic repercussions, they may be more open to your counseling their child.

While psychological counseling may be difficult to dispense, be free with advice. As a teacher, counselor, or administrator the student will respect your opinion, as will the parents. Be open with students and parents about discussing local social ills such as the availability of drugs, places to avoid "hanging out," and the advances of the opposite sex. These topics might be off limits for "good boys and girls" at home, and the teacher or counselor might be the only adult who can give a Western perspective. If the students are coming directly from Korea, where these social ills are more hidden, they might be simply naive. Conversely, smoking and excessive drinking is a regular rite of passage for Korean males upon (and now even before) high school graduation. The health hazards of smoking and drunkenness are understood but widely ignored in Korea. Junior may possibly be just following dad's example in these areas.

8. Understand that students may be studying a parallel Korean curriculum. As mentioned earlier, success in the Western school, while important, may not be as crucial to their future as keeping up with Korean studies. Involvement in extracurricular school activities will get them nowhere in Korea when they return. Looking at this from a strictly Western perspective is potentially harmful to the students if their futures lie in Korea. Candid discussion with the family as to their child's eventual educational future may be in order. If the child's future is in Western higher education, parents should be advised that a more Western-style "well-rounded" education will be necessary, possibly at the loss of some advancement in Korean education. A child simply cannot do both with 100% effort. Some priorities must be set, but remember that they might not be yours!

9. Emphasize involvement in extra-curricular activities. Unless the child is simply too busy with Korean studies, he or she should be strongly encouraged to join clubs, play sports, get involved in music, and attend dances, if for no other reason than to have greater exposure to English out of the classroom. Parents may see these activities as a waste of time, whereas we see them as part of a well-rounded education. This needs to be emphasized to both parents and students, especially if the child is headed to a Western university where emphasis is placed on such activities and college admissions may rest on a record of involvement in activities.

10. Learn to interpret Korean body language and manners. As anyone who has worked interculturally knows, body language and manners are almost as different between cultures as is spoken language. Here are some common examples:

- *Respect towards superiors in Korea is demonstrated by having downcast eyes and a slightly bowed head.* Saying "Look me in the eye when I talk to you!" may put the child in a real dilemma — it's like telling an American child to look the other way when spoken to! Especially when being scolded this stance is apparent. Looking someone directly in the eyes in Korea is aggressive and confrontational. Not understanding this can be frustrating to the Western teacher and frightening to the child!.

- *When being scolded, children will remain quiet.* Asking questions like "Why did you hit Susie?" will more often result in silence and the accompanying bowed head than in an answer. This is a stance of submission and shame, not defiance. If a teacher really wants to know why Tae-jin hit Susie, she should sit down with the child later and ask quietly. An answer still might not be immediately forthcoming, but the chances of eventually finding out what happened are at least greater.

- *Giggles or laughter often accompany embarrassment.* This is one of the most frustrating behaviors for Westerners living in Korea to get used to — it's pretty irritating to ask a question, fall down, or do something embarrassing and be met with laughter! Understanding this may help — but it will take a real effort. Adolescent Korean girls are particularly adept at giggling behind a demurely held handkerchief.

- *It's better to sniffle through a class than blow the nose.* In Korea, it's acceptable (for an older person) to belch loudly, to hungrily slurp one's noodles, and to sniffle forever — but really honking the nose is unacceptable! (If you honk, plan on hearing some of those embarrassed giggles!) Even a discreet and quiet blowing of the nose gets attention. Especially with young children, have a box of tissue handy in the classroom and be sure they know that they're expected to use it. Westerners who visit a Korean home or Korean restaurant would be advised to leave the room before blowing the nose — and then do it quietly. Sneezes are likewise not responded to with a "Bless you!" The thinking goes "Of course I am embarrassed to make such a noise. Why embarrass myself more by calling attention to it? Why, too, should I apologize after sneezing and thus further disrupt the class?"

- *be prepared to have a door swung closed in your face*. Everyone who has ever lived in Korea has approached the swinging supermarket door, arms full of bundles, and have a person breeze through the door ahead of them and let it swing shut in their face. Holding a door open for a stranger simply has not become part of the "manner set" in Korean yet. This is related to the importance of relationships; a person would never think of *not* holding a door (and even carrying the bags of groceries) of someone they knew personally.

- *"Thank you," "I'm sorry," and "You're welcome" may not be used as often as you may expect*. There are perfectly good words for these expressions in Korean, but they are just not used very often. Korea is a "high context" culture — lots of what is communicated is not spoken directly. Of course a person is thankful to you or feels regret, but it simply is often not verbalized. You are expected to understand that they feel this way, and there is no need for them to point it out verbally.

Should the school try to understand these behaviors? Of course. It is always good to understand that other cultures have different manners and codes of behavior. But should they be accepted as normal in a Western-style school? I don't think so. We should teach Western manners as we would anything else — tools that work in another culture. Just as we teach appropriate language for use in Western settings, we should teach appropriate Western etiquette. Knowing appropriate behaviors in particular situations is the key to survival in any culture. Your learning to use some Korean manners with them will encourage them to learn to use Western manners with you and other Westerners, and will send the message to students that you do not consider Korean manners to be "bad," but just inappropriate in a Western setting. The key here is to use situationally appropriate codes of conduct, as long as they don't conflict with deeper moral or ethical codes.

11. Beware of issues of hierarchy, "face," and "respect." These are major issues among ethnic Korean children in international schools, and should be dealt with head-on by the school. As discussed earlier, Confucianism is a two-way street: respect and obedience by younger towards older, and protection and care by older of younger. Unfortunately, too often only the first half of this equation is practiced. Among both boys and girls, there is a strong hierarchy, mostly based on grade in school and age. Students younger by even one year refer to their older compatriots as their "seniors" and use the common Korean words for older brother ("hyung" or "o-pa") and for older sister ("noo-na" or

129

"uhn-yi.") They look up to them, they do their bidding, and they are all too often abused by them. Most older students genuinely care about their younger "brothers and sisters," as long as the younger ones treat them with outward respect. This can take the form of expecting from a younger student a simple nod of the head in the hallway (a common Korean greeting), or it can escalate to a forced purchase of lunch, demands to run errands, or orders to do other even more menial tasks. Students should know that "Confucius was not a bully!" Of course, the more confident, secure, and mature an older student is, the less demeaning his or her expectations are. However, to the insecure young person (or to the plain old bully) it is a socially acceptable system too good to be true. The price a younger student pays for not going along with this system is all too often physical abuse, threats, and intimidation. In Korea, it often results in serious psychological or physical harm, and when a student feels helpless to do anything about it, even in suicide. Although this type of bullying is decried in Korean society, it is also accepted as "the way things are," for Korea *is* a nation steeped in hierarchy and special respect towards those higher up the social or political ladder. Parents tell their children that they should respect their "elders," and that if it gets too rough they should just go along with it. It is a rite of passage and an unfortunate aspect of acculturation.

Particularly vulnerable to this type of abuse is an ethnic Korean child who was not brought up in Korea or in a Korean community and who is not aware of the rules of this game in his or her new school. It is all too easy for them to look at or speak to an older student too casually, to not bow deeply enough, or to offend the wrong person. Such newcomers will be "educated" as to their errant behavior, and if they don't get the message quickly they may be more forcefully indoctrinated into the realities of Korean social norms. Korean-style intimidation may go on right in front of the unsuspecting Western eyes, and unless the school has built a strong culture among students of not tolerating bullying, it will seldom be reported by either students or parents. As parents are often at the root of this behavior by encouraging what Westerners might consider excess "respect," parent groups must be involved in the solution if this becomes a widespread problem. A Westerner trying to step in, unless he or she truly understands the nature of the structure and has the trust of the Korean community, will only be seen as a meddling foreigner who just "doesn't respect our culture." Don't fall for this reasoning. Bullying is bullying! Fortunately, this type of subservient behavior is seldom expected of younger non-Koreans.

Remember that whenever there are more than a few Korean students in a school, particularly if they are in different grades, it is not a question of *whether* a hierarchy exists — it naturally exists. The real questions we need to ask ourselves are these: "In our school, has this behavior become negative? Is it dangerous? Are some children afraid to come to school because of it? Is our school really the physically and emotionally safe place we think it is for *all* our students? Are we ignoring real danger to students because of our fear of treading on tender cultural toes?" We need to be willing to "call a bully a bully" in any language and in any culture. This is an example of where our desire to be culturally sensitive must be overcome by our more deeply held values of having a school that is safe and free of harassment.

Interestingly, this sense of hierarchy also exists in the parent community, with adult-level signs of respect and subservience expected. In a small expatriate Korean community overseas made up of employees from the same company, it may follow the ranking in that organization. Not unlike a military community, where a general is clearly superior to a colonel and so on down the line, a company has the same strict levels. Also not unlike the military, the spouses (normally the wives) have a parallel hierarchy, with the company manager's wife enjoying a higher position than that of the chief engineer's wife, etc. When such a built-in structure is not already in place, a hierarchy will quickly form, often according to the age of the parents, what university they attended, or what year they graduated from university. This parental hierarchy can be of real help to the school when the school is trying to get the community to buy into a program or carry out some change. If the top of the social structure is identified and is won over, half the battle is won. It would be very difficult for those of lower social standing to assume a leadership position or speak out against a social "superior."

12. Celebrate biculturalism. Young people of middle or high school age struggle with their emerging identities in the best of situations. Given a cross cultural situation in which they may be getting very different messages about who they are from their friends, from the school, from parents, from family back home, and from their own fragile egos, confusion can reign. It is natural that in the process of adjusting from a secure cultural identity to one of some cultural ambiguity young people (and adults, as well) may swing from one extreme to another. Korean children who have just moved overseas (or a Korean-American who has just moved to Korea) may try to fit into their new youth culture as quickly as possible in order to be accepted. They may quickly adopt extremes in dress, language, or habits in the new culture, but later on may feel that they are being disloyal to their old culture and swing back, identifying themselves, for example, as "super-Americans" or "super-Koreans" depending on their situations. Neither of these extremes is very attractive. Students need to know that their ability to move easily from one culture to another depending on whom they are talking to or whose home they are in is not being disloyal to anyone or any nation; it is a gift that will give them greater flexibility in life later on, and may even bring them real financial and career advantages. Kids need to be given psychological permission to be bicultural. Celebrate biculturalism in your school!

13. Suggest or provide early re-entry counseling. Whether a child is returning to Korea from abroad or leaving Korea after a temporary stay, the re-entry adjustment will be difficult. Most readers are aware of ways to assist students in moving "back" to their "home" country, even if they have never lived there. Pollock and Van Reken (see reference list) give tremendous insight into the challenges of such a move.

Finally, again remember that all of these generalities are just that -- general characteristics. Each parent, family, and child is unique in background, in history, in values, and in plans for the future. Use the information in this book as a guide, understanding that no family will fit these characteristics completely. Don't make any assumptions. It is just as dangerous to assume that a Korean child or parent will exhibit all of these characteristics as it is to assume that they are totally Westernized. Take time to get to know each student and family. Give each young person a chance to be an *individual* — one whose uniqueness is a developing mosaic of both Asian and Western experiences. That is a gift that can never be taken away from them. It is also their special gift to you!

Looking Back, Looking Ahead

Is your school doing any of the things suggested above to help ethnic Korean students adjust to your school? Why or why not? What is your counseling department doing to help students prepare for re-entry to Korea?

Is there a hidden bullying problem in your school? Do fights seem to erupt for reasons that seem silly to you – often matters of "respect"? Are your ethnic Korean students forming exclusive cliques? If so, are the cliques harmful?

Have you ever thought, "These kids are so nice they would never cheat in my class?" Is your policy on plagiarism consciously taught to your students, and enforced?

What are you doing to help students feel free to ask questions in class? What are you doing to encourage independent thinking? Are you rewarding it when you get it?

Are there girls who are holding back and not participating? What can you do about it?

CHAPTER IX: FROM TEACHERS . . .

Perhaps the best help to you, the teacher, is to hear what other teachers have had to say. Below are some comments made experienced teachers of ethnic Korean students working at international schools in Korea. Read them now, and again in a month or so. See if you agree with these teachers.

"Find ways to encourage students to learn for pleasure, such as the joy which comes from finishing a mystery novel, rather than the pressure to achieve high grades . . . "

"Enjoy the hard-working, respectful and disciplined nature of the students, but be prepared to be somewhat frustrated by their reluctance to enter actively into student-centered activities and creative thinking . . ."

"It's more important to teach them how to be independent, learn for knowledge, and how to have fun. Their parents will make sure they get 'the grades,' but they need a teacher to show them the other 'realities' and fun aspects of life . . . "

"Whatever the reason, the students produce an environment of 'stress' to keep themselves motivated. Don't get trapped in that environment . . . "

"Make frequent home contact. The parents are very friendly and helpful."

"They see through Korean and to some extent American eyes and are constantly juggling the two in their daily encounters at school."

"... Korean-American students tend to be quiet in class, especially girls. This is not an indication that they don't know what is going on or are disinterested. It's their upbringing; they are taught to be passive in front of adults."

"We should attempt to balance the high expectations of parents/students with a program that bolsters self-esteem and encourages acceptance of more realistic goals . . . "

"One of the things that has helped me has been an understanding of the tendency [among ethnic Koreans] to view things in a black/white, ordinal, hierarchical way. I have found that frustrating in communicating with parents at times . . . "

"Understand Korean culture. . . understand Korean culture . . . understand Korean culture . . . "

"Never assume you've arrived —that now you understand the students or their parents. Remember that you are looking at the world through a very different set of historical and cultural lenses than their parents are, and you will therefore never share the same perception of reality with them."

And finally,

"Especially if you've never worked with Asian (Korean-American) students, come with a clean slate and NO preconceived ideas. Be ready to be shocked, excited, frustrated, challenged. They will work hard, they will give you honor, they will over-achieve, they will push for extra points in their grade, their behavior will confound you and sometimes frustrate you. At the end of the day (year) you will have a sense of accomplishment and pride in the education that has happened in your classroom."

SUGGESTED READINGS

To better understand the cultural and sociological challenges facing the children of Asian immigrants in the United States, see *Growing Up Asian American: An Anthology* (1993), edited by Maria Hong (New York: William Morrow). Not limited to Korean emigrants, this anthology samples Asian-American literature from the early part of the Twentieth Century to the present. Another excellent collection of stories describing what it means to be an Asian American is found in *Asian American Experiences in the United States* (1991) by J. Lee (Jefferson, NC: McFarland & Co.). Of particular interest are sections by Charles Ryu, a Korean-American pastor living in New York. A section dealing with the "1.5 generation" is particularly relevant. An anthology of 38 fascinating Korean-American immigrant stories is found in *East to America* (1996) by Elaine H. Kim and Eui-Young Yu (New York: The New Press). An historical novel tracing the actual life of the author's Korean grandmother during the Japanese occupation and the Korean War is *Still Life with Rice* (1996) by Helie Lee (New York: Simon & Schuster).

Few resources about the ethnic Asian student in America are quite so prescriptive, descriptive, and insightful as the *Handbook for Teaching Korean-American Students* (1992) by the Bilingual Education Office, California Department of Education (Sacramento, CA). This book was prepared to assist educators in understanding and helping immigrant Korean children and parents adjust to American culture and education. The background of Korean-Americans in California, educational and sociological issues accompanying immigration, the impact of the Korean language and educational system on immigrant issues, recommended instructional and curricular strategies, and an extensive bibliography are included. Available from California Dept. of Education, P.O. Box 271, Sacramento, CA 95812-0271, U.S.A.

A quick primer in Korean social customs, especially those that cause comment and sometimes discomfort among non-Koreans (particularly Americans), is *Ugly Koreans, Ugly Americans* (1995) by Min, Byoung-chul (Seoul: BCM Publishers). While the cartoons in this book are somewhat stereotypical of Asians and Westerners, the reader can learn a good deal about how not to offend (and how not to be offended by) Koreans who may not have spent much time in the West (A similar book, *Ugly Japanese, Ugly Americans*, is published by the same author).

Another valuable resource for understanding Korean culture is *Culture Shock: Korea* by S. Hur and B. Hur (Graphic Arts Center Publishing Co., 2002)

For a broad, unbiased, and enjoyable trip through Korean history and culture from prehistoric times to the present read *Korea's Place in the Sun* (1997), by Bruce Cumings (New York: W. W. Norton & Co.) For a close-up look at recent Korean history from a British perspective, *The Koreans: Who They Are, What they Want, Where Their Future Lies* (1998) by Michael Breen (London: Orion Business Books) is informative and insightful. An excellent history of both North and South Korea is found in *The Two Koreas: A Contemporary History* (1997), by Don Oberdorfer (Reading, MA: Addison-Wesley). There are any number of "I was there" genre Korean War books on the market, but certainly one of the very best all-round histories of the war is *In Mortal Combat: Korea, 1950-1953* (1991) by John Toland (New York: William Morrow and Company). For a Korean perspective on the war, *From Pusan to Panmunjom* (1992), by General Paik Sun Yup is very readable (Dulles, Virginia: Brassey's). For a true tale of the horrors of being a North Korean prisoner during the war, read Larry Zeller's first-hand account of three years in captivity, *In Enemy Hands* (The University Press of Kentucky, 1991). There are many other excellent books about Korean history and culture the market.

For up-to-date information on Korea contact the Korean embassy or consulate in your city. Many larger cities have offices of the Korea National Tourism Corporation, which publishes excellent materials, most of which are free. The Korean government and the Seoul City government also maintain extensive web pages.

An excellent resource for those who counsel non-North American or non-European students is *Counseling the Culturally Different: Theory and Practice* (2nd ed.), (1990) by Derald Sue and David Sue (New York: John Wiley & Sons). The premier book on children growing up outside their own culture as Third Culture Kids is *The Third Culture Kid Experience: Growing Up among Worlds* (1999) by David Pollock and Ruth E. Van Reken (Yarmouth, Maine: Intercultural Press, Inc.). This book is one of a kind, and is "a must" for any former, present, or future Third Culture Kid or their parents or spouse, as well as for educators working with TCK's. A touching and sensitive "child's eye view" of being an Asian missionary child is found in *Kids without Borders: Journals of Chinese Missionary Kids*, edited by Helen Loong (OMF Hong Kong and Hong Kong Association of Christian Missions, 2000).

REFERENCE LIST

The following resources were noted in the text:

Cultural factors on trial at Korean Air crash inquiry. (1988, March 28). The Korea Herald .

Cumings, Bruce. (1997). *Korea's Place in the Sun.* (New York: W. W. Norton & Co.)

Handbook for Teaching Korean-American Students. (1992). (Sacramento, CA: Bilingual Education Office, California Department of Education).

Kim, Young-kwon (Ed.) *A Handbook of Korea, 1978.* (Seoul: Korean Overseas Information Service, Ministry of Culture and Information).

Kohls, L. Robert. (1996). *Survival Kit for Overseas Living* (3rd ed.) (Yarmouth, ME: Intercultural Press, Inc.).

Noh, Sung Eun. (1988). *Returned Korean Immigrant Children's Perceptions about Their Educational Environments in Korea.* (Doctoral Dissertation, Univ. of Connecticut).

Pollock, David, and Ruth E. Van Reken. (1999). *The Third Culture Kid Experience: Growing Up among Worlds.* (Yarmouth, Maine: Intercultural Press, Inc.).

Shin, H. S. (1997, November 18). *Tomorrow's college entrance exam educational event of the year.* The Korea Herald

Shin, H. S. (1997, November 20). *College entrance exam held nationwide. The Korea Herald.*

Statistical Handbook of Korea, 2002; http://www.nso.go.kr/eng/

Sue, David and D. Sue. (1990). *Counseling the Culturally Different: Theory and Practice* (2nd ed.). (New York: John Wiley & Sons).

Understanding A Western Education: A Guide for Parents & Students (undated). (Taejon, Korea: Taejon Christian International School, <tcisinfo@tcis.or.kr>).

A (VERY) BRIEF LEXICON OF KOREAN EDUCATIONAL TERMS . . .

Most ethnic Korean parents speak some English, and some speak excellent English, but some speak none at all, although written skills are usually much better. However, if you are calling a student's home and cannot seem to make yourself understood, you might want to walk on the thin ice of trying a few words and phrases of educational Korean. *Try to pronounce each syllable without an accent.*

Hak-seng	student
Hak-yo	school
Sun-seng	teacher
Sahng-dahm sun-seng	counselor
Kyo-jhang sun-seng	principal
Kong-boo	study
Sook-jae	homework
Cho-ah-yo	good
An-cho-ah-yo	not good
Soo-hak	math
Kwa-hak	science
Sah-wheh	social studies
Cheh-yook	physical education
Uhm-ak	music
Mee-sool	art
Young-uh	English language

Some useful phrases:

"This is (I am) Min-soo's English teacher.":
(Student's name) + (subject name)+ sun-seng+ im-ni-da.

EX: "I am Min-soo's English teacher" = "Min-soo's English teacher (I) am." : *"Min-soo young-uh son-seng imnida."*

(Name) chal hess-uh-yo.	(Name) did well.
(Min-soo chal hess-uh-yo.)	
Mi-ahn-hahm-ni-da	I'm sorry!
An-ni-oh	No
Yeh or *Neh*	Yes
Kahm-sah-hahm-ni-da!	Thank you!

ABOUT THE AUTHOR

Jonathan Borden has lived in Korea since 1975. After a brief stint as a missionary volunteer on the southern island of Kojedo, he began teaching at Seoul Foreign School, an international school serving expatriate children from forty-nine nations who are living in Seoul. While at Seoul Foreign School he has taught elementary, middle, and high school grades, and has been secondary and middle school principal. During this time he has gotten to know thousands of ethnic Korean students and parents from all types of backgrounds. It has been a labor of love.

Dr. Borden lives in Seoul with his Korean-born educator wife, Soon-ok. They have two sons, TCK's born in Korea and products of Seoul Foreign School and the international community.

Dr. Borden received his doctorate from Walden University, where he concentrated on early adolescent and intercultural (particularly Korean/American) education. He and his wife lead workshops on the subject of ethnic Korean children and parents at international schools and at international educational conferences.

NOTES